Par and Yardage

Hole	Par	Yardage	Hole	Par	Yardage
1	4	381	10	4	446
2	4	484	11	4	380
3	4	390	12	3	202
4	4	331	13	4	406
5	3	188	14	5	573
6	5	524	15	4	397
7	3	106	16	4	403
8	4	418	17	3	208
9	4	466	18	5	543
	35	3,288		36	3,558
				71	6,846

Writer: Robert Sommers   Photographers: Michael Cohen, Fred Vuich   Editor: Bev Norwood

ISBN 1-878843-29-X

©2000 United States Golf Association®
Golf House, Far Hills, N.J. 07931

Statistics produced by Unisys Corporation

Course illustrations by Libby Peper (holes 1-4, 6-18) and
Dan Wardlaw (hole 5 and course map) © The Majors of Golf

Published by IMG Worldwide Inc.,
1360 East Ninth Street, Cleveland, Ohio 44114

Designed and produced by Davis Design

Printed in the United States of America

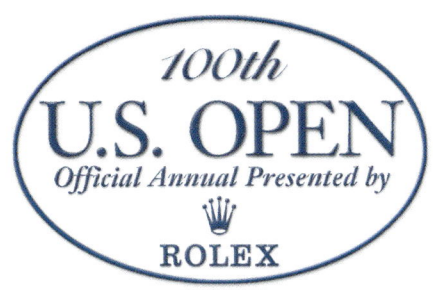

Win a United States Open Championship by 15 strokes on a golf course as demanding as Pebble Beach? Awesome. Surprising? Well, in a way, yes, but not entirely. I had a pretty good idea of what Tiger Woods was capable of accomplishing as a professional before he became one, and not just from the common knowledge of his remarkable amateur career. I played a practice round with Tiger at Augusta National the week of the 1996 Masters, and what I saw convinced me that we had a new superstar on the horizon.

I hadn't seen a young man with that much talent, poise and determination since I encountered Jack Nicklaus before he launched his brilliant professional career. Furthermore, he has shown me over these last few years that he personifies something my father impressed upon me at an early age about golf — that it is a game 90 percent of which is played from the shoulders up.

What Tiger can accomplish in the future could well exceed any limits we might think now exist. Besides, his influence on the game transcends birdies and eagles and the victories themselves. He is bringing so many newcomers to the game, many as players and many more as followers. People who never paid any attention to the game are interested and enthusiastic about what he is doing, and golf is benefitting from that.

I commend to you this detailed official account of Tiger Woods' historic victory in the 2000 U.S. Open that Rolex and the United States Golf Association present in this 16th annual commemorative book.

Arnold Palmer

The seventh hole, par 3 and 106 yards.

Strange, isn't it, how some real estate ventures that don't work out, work out for the best?

Take Pebble Beach. If the Pacific Improvement Company had followed through with its plans, Tiger Woods wouldn't have won the 100th U.S. Open over this magnificent golf course in June 2000. Oh, he would have won, of course — he would have won if it had been played through Death Valley or straight down Ocean Avenue in Carmel. But there would have been no glorious march along this special 18th fairway while crowds cheered and waves lapped against the rocks. No, the shoreline would have been crammed with houses built on 50-foot lots along the bluffs overlooking the Pacific.

The land turned out as it did because Pacific Improvement's interests changed, and the directors assigned Sam Morse, one of its employees, to dispose of the property. With an eye for the rugged beauty of the country, as well as for a sound investment, Morse, a shrewd man, disposed of it by forming Del Monte Properties and buying it himself.

The grand nephew and namesake of Samuel F.B. Morse, the inventor of the telegraph and Morse Code, young Sam was brought into the company because he had been a classmate of Charles Crocker's grandson at Yale.

Crocker was a powerful man in California. He was a partner of Leland Stanford, Collis Huntington and Mark Hopkins, the four men who organized and built the Central Pacific Railroad, which linked with the Union Pacific in 1869 and completed the first transcontinental railroad.

While Stanford, the governor of California, and Huntington, who based himself in Washington, took care of political matters and Hopkins, the financial wizard, handled the money, Crocker personally took on the actual construction. Bringing in Chinese workers, he drove the line from Sacramento through the mountains and on to Utah at a remarkable rate, in half the time allotted by the federal government. The Central Pacific met the Union Pacific at Promontory Point, Utah, in May 1869.

The four men became enormously wealthy and accumulated vast real estate holdings, including about 7,000 acres near Monterey, about 90 miles south of San Francisco.

An unusually cosmopolitan region, peopled first by Native Americans and later by gold-lusting Spanish invaders, Japanese divers harvesting abalone from the sea bed, Russian fur traders ravishing the sea otter colonies, New England whalers, salmon fishermen of all kinds, a wave of Sicilian fishermen, Anglo cattle ranchers and truck farmers of all descriptions, Monterey had been the capital of both Spanish and Mexican California. Robert Louis Stevenson wrote some of his stories there, John Steinbeck gave us *Cannery Row* and *The Grapes of Wrath*, and Robinson Jeffers composed darkly passionate poetry from his castle beside the shore, built from rocks he hauled up from the beach.

Into this atmosphere, Pacific Improvement began developing a resort in the 1880s. First came the Del Monte Hotel, a massive structure with 500 rooms, then a golf course in the 1890s. A spur railroad ran two trains a day down from San Francisco, and the resort flourished.

As the years passed, Crocker, Hopkins, Hun-

Pebble Beach

tington and Stanford died, and Pacific Improvement lost interest in developing what had become the Del Monte Forest. This, of course, led to Morse's decision to buy the land.

In control now, Morse changed the concept of Pebble Beach. Instead of a coast lined with houses, he imagined golf holes running along those craggy headlands. But he had a problem. Pacific Improvement had sold 80 of those 50-foot building lots. A supreme salesman, Morse persuaded all but three owners to sell. Laid out by Jack Neville and Douglas Grant, two amateur golfers with no experience in golf architecture, Morse's dream has stood among the game's superbly designed tests since it opened in 1919.

1st
PAR 4
381 YARDS

of just over 500 yards. Protected in front by a wide barranca and to the left by a pair of live oaks, it was reached routinely by tournament-class golfers with second shots played with irons.

As the 2000 Open approached, pitch canker, which had been ravaging California forests, claimed one of the oaks, eliminating one obstacle, and with the distances the modern tournament golfer hits the ball, the USGA shortened the second hole to 484 yards and reclassified it as a par 4. When some golfers objected, claiming the change defied tradition and gave them no means of comparing themselves with those from the past, they were reminded they were no longer playing persimmon woods with steel shafts and wound balata balls with 342 dimples. Once the championship began and 5- and 6-irons became the common club of choice for second shots, no one mentioned tradition.

From there the course turns toward the ocean with a doglegged par 4, then begins a seven-hole march along the seafront with the fourth, a short par 4 of 331 yards.

2nd
PAR 4
484 YARDS

In all of golf there is nothing quite like Pebble Beach. It demands everything of a golfer — power, finesse, intense concentration. It has short par 4s, long par 4s, four par 3s that range from 106 yards to over 200 yards, and three par 5s that might be reached with the second shot but that carry risks not many golfers are willing to take. Half its holes skirt the twisting shoreline, where the ocean pounds against sheer cliffs that may plummet 50 feet to the blue water below.

For the golfer, those features lie ahead, for instead of opening with a big bang, Pebble Beach eases into the round with the first three holes, two mild par 4s and another, the second, that stirred some controversy for the 2000 Open. Since its beginnings, the second hole had been designated a par 5, although a very easy par 5

3rd
PAR 4
390 YARDS

100th U.S. Open

The third hole, par 4 and 390 yards.

Pebble Beach

The fourth hole, par 4 and 331 yards.

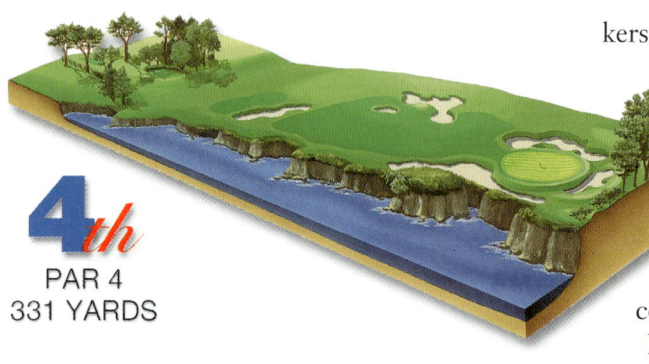

4th
PAR 4
331 YARDS

Now it moves to the fifth, the first entirely new hole since the original design, covering the ground Morse coveted but couldn't buy. Pebble Beach took over the tract when survivors of the original owners finally decided to sell.

The original fifth simply didn't fit the flow of the course; it turned inland, away from the sea to an uphill green blind to the tee shot. With the new property in hand, Pebble Beach called on the Jack Nicklaus group to design a new par 3 along the shoreline.

It turned out to be an infinitely better hole than the original. Measuring 188 yards, it perches on the edge of a cliff, its green guarded by bunkers on the right front and left rear and canted to feed the ball toward the right rear. Shots that dive into the scraggly rough can easily cost a stroke or two. Besides, the timid tend to play well left to avoid the beach, guaranteeing a bogey at best. This is a very hard hole, a marvelous addition to a classic course.

Beginning with the fifth you are playing golf of the most demanding order, each shot flirting with the cliffs along the ocean shore.

5th
PAR 3
188 YARDS

8

100th U.S. Open

The fifth hole, par 3 and 188 yards.

Next the course moves to the sixth, a shortish par 5 of 513 yards that rises to a high escarpment above Stillwater Cove, which in earlier times had been a settlement of Chinese fishermen but evolved into a yacht basin. The course then pitches downward to a rocky shelf at the edge of Carmel Bay with the 106-yard seventh, a frightening little par 3 played from a high tee to a tiny green ringed with bunkers.

In calm weather the tee shot is no more than a wedge, but when the wind whips in from the Pacific, it could call for a long iron. Playing in the Bing Crosby Pro-Am some years earlier, Ken Venturi played a full-blooded 3-iron. During the blustery last day of the 1992 Open, hardly anyone hit the green. Most punched 4-, 5- or 6-irons, trying to bore through the wind, and Scott Simpson tried a pitching club instead. Played into the teeth of the gale, the shot made little progress toward the green, but no one had seen a ball climb higher. With Nick Faldo approaching, some fans decided to wait for him, figuring he would know how to play the shot since he was then at the peak of his game. He overshot the green and double-bogeyed.

6th
PAR 5
524 YARDS

7th
PAR 3
106 YARDS

9

Pebble Beach

The ninth hole, par 4 and 466 yards.

100th U.S. Open

Moving on, no hole could be more intimidating than the eighth, a 418-yard par 4 that begins at the base of the slope that leads downward to the seventh green. The tee shot is blind, back up the grade to the crest of a plateau, and it must be played with great control, not only for direction but for distance as well. A drive that flies too far could drop off the edge of a savage chasm that drops 80 feet straight down to a cove where waves churn against the gray cliffs. While the fairway swings left and serpentines around the head of the cove, the green is off to the right.

The approach must be played across the gorge to a tiny green set among deep and punishing bunkers. Let the shot leak to the right and the ball could fall to the beach; play too timidly and it could ricochet off the rocky bluff and into the sea. Make sure of the carry and go beyond the green and you are in pretty bad shape there, too, for now you must play your third shot back toward the cliff's edge.

The eighth hole, in short, is a magnificent test of nerves and skill. It just might be the best par-4 hole in all of golf. If not that, along with the ninth and 10th, it is one-third of the game's most demanding series of three holes.

Both the ninth and 10th follow the edge of the cliffs over land that pitches and rolls and tends to kick the ball toward the sea. At 466 yards, the ninth is the longer of the two and its fairway the wider. Two steep-faced bunkers sit left of the fairway beginning about 250 yards out and running for perhaps 20 yards. At this point the fairway is little more than 30 yards wide. With the fairway tilting toward the bluffs, this is a testing tee shot, indeed. The natural tendency is to stay away from the right and the plunge down to the beach, but the bunkers to the left are difficult because of their high frontal walls.

At 446 yards, the 10th is shorter, but many of its problems mirror those of the ninth. Its fairway is set up narrower than the ninth's around the area of the fairway bunker, which is much larger and elongated, and its green is more closely guarded, not only by bunkers, but by a depression on the right covered with thick grass. It was there in 1982 that Tom Watson nearly lost the Open, but from thick kikuyu grass, he chopped his ball onto the green and saved his par. Ten years earlier a gust of wind had caught Nicklaus at the top of his backswing, blew his driver off line, and he drove onto the beach, costing him a double bogey. He won, nevertheless.

You are now at the outer reaches of the course. From there it runs inland, weaving among the cypress, eucalyptus, live oaks and Monterey pines before returning to the sea once again at the 17th, a par 3 with an hourglass-shaped green set at an angle to the line of flight, bordered on three sides by bunkers, and with the rocky coastline just beyond and to the left, where so many fine rounds have

8th
PAR 4
418 YARDS

9th
PAR 4
466 YARDS

10th
PAR 4
446 YARDS

11

Pebble Beach

been shattered by a misplayed shot.

It was there, too, that two unforgettable shots were played in the Open's last rounds. Nicklaus opened his lead over Bruce Crampton to four strokes with a 1-iron shot that rattled the flagstick in 1972, and Watson ended Nicklaus' dream of a fifth Open by pitching in from the left rough for a birdie 2 in 1982 while Nicklaus watched on a television screen in the scorer's tent.

Then there's the 18th, a glorious finishing hole along the coast. Measuring 543 yards for the 2000 Open, it has nearly everything golf-course designing has up its sleeve. Sparkling in the sunlight, Carmel Bay lies to the left, out of bounds lines the right, two Monterey pines stand as a target on the right where a good drive should settle, and more trees block an approach played from too far right. Bunkers nearly encircle the green, leaving a narrow chute in the front.

Allowed to shore up the coastline with concrete barriers shaped and colored like natural rocks a year or so before the 2000 Open, Pebble Beach took advantage and added about 750 square feet to the back left of the green and extended the teeing ground farther into the bay.

Like the 14th, the 18th is a true three-shot hole. Should a player come to the home hole needing to make up a shot, he would run great risks going for the green with his second. It has been done, though. Certainly by Tiger Woods in the Pebble Beach National Pro-Am.

Its perils aside, Pebble Beach is a joy to play.

11th PAR 4 380 YARDS

12th PAR 3 202 YARDS

It is the most scenically spectacular of all those sites where the great championships are played. New South Wales, near Sydney, Australia, may rival its setting, and Ballybunion, in Ireland, and Turnberry, in Scotland, have a number of stunning holes along the Atlantic, but neither approaches the overall character, the majesty or the scale of Pebble Beach.

Looking outward from Pebble Beach's craggy headlands, Point Lobos hides in a ghostly mist, while closer in sea lions bark on rocky outcroppings offshore and black cormorants spread their wings to dry nearby. Nearly extinct sea otters float among the kelp, feasting on sea urchins they crack open by beating stones against them as they're cradled on their bellies. The setting often takes the mind away from the demands of the game.

Since its introduction to the Open in 1972, the quality of the players who have won there has shown the wisdom of Pebble Beach as the site of the national championship. With the 2000 playing, Pebble Beach has seen four Opens. Three of them have been won by the best players of their time — Nicklaus in 1972, Watson in 1982 and now Woods, who set a standard that may last a lifetime. Tom Kite, the 1992 champion, was a fine player as well, a consistent force in the game for 20 years.

While Nicklaus, Watson and Kite had each played one memorable shot in his fourth round (Kite holed a pitch from behind the seventh for a birdie 2), by finishing 15 strokes ahead of the field, Woods left behind no one particular shot, although his 200-yard 7-iron into the sixth was something to behold.

100th U.S. Open

The 10th hole, par 4 and 446 yards, and the 11th hole, par 4 and 380 yards.

Pebble Beach

Like most of our great courses, Pebble Beach has been strengthened and refined a few times since it opened shortly after the First World War. The 18th hole, for example, which so many authorities consider the best closing hole in golf, began as a 350-yard par 4 of no great character, but in stages it became a wonderful par 5.

A number of men had a hand in the changes. Chandler Egan, the 1904 and 1905 U.S. Amateur champion, did most of the heavy work preparing Pebble Beach for the 1929 U.S. Amateur, and others contributed refinements as well. Robert Hunter, a disciple of Alister Mackenzie, had a hand in it, as well as Mackenzie himself, and Herbert Fowler, a prominent British architect, rebuilt the 18th for the 1922 season. First he brought the tee closer to the bay, setting it on a small promontory at the water's edge, then he pushed the green farther back and closer to the brink of the bay.

Later, Egan re-shaped and re-bunkered every green, creating the impression of dunesland. When he had finished with the seventh, it looked like an oasis in the Sahara, just a dot of green among the white sand.

As Pebble Beach's character changed, so did its ownership. In order to buy the property originally, Morse had brought in Herbert Fleishhacker, the president of the Anglo Bank of San Francisco, but when the Great Depression struck, Fleishhacker went bankrupt.

13th PAR 4 406 YARDS

Somehow, Morse put together enough money to buy a substantial part of Fleishhacker's holdings and took control.

Known as the Duke of Del Monte, Morse ruled Del Monte Properties through the following three decades. He died in 1969. Fourteen years later, in 1983, ownership passed to Miller, Klutznick, Davis and Gray, a real estate partnership headed by Marvin Davis, a powerful man in the oil business. The group also owned the 20th Century Fox film studio.

Davis had so little interest in golf that almost as soon as his group bought it, he decided to sell.

14th PAR 5 573 YARDS

By then the Japanese seemed to have all the money in the world. Their economy was purring along in high gear and their management techniques were envied throughout the financial and industrial world.

And they loved golf. They had built enclosed driving ranges throughout the country, which became the only taste of golf some fanatics would ever savor, and the occasional zealot who could not afford the obscene million dollar initiation fees some clubs demanded would fly to the Philippines for a weekend game.

This is how Minoru Isutani entered the picture in 1990. A developer of real estate and owner of a number of

15th PAR 4 397 YARDS

100th U.S. Open

The 13th hole, par 4 and 406 yards.

Pebble Beach

golf clubs, Isutani went looking for an American trophy. He found it in Pebble Beach and all the property and hotels that by now made up the company.

There is a priceless vignette of what is said to have happened when Isutani and Davis met to work out the sale. Davis evidently lived to negotiate. He loved it; it kept him alive. His group had bought the property for a little more than $80 million, so to have his fun, Davis decided he'd ask more than 10 times his buying price.

A big man, standing well over six feet tall and quite heavy, Davis dwarfed Isutani. Sitting across the table, he threw out the figure of $841 million, expecting a fun battle as they worked down to a reasonable figure.

Instead, with a serene smile, Isutani reached into his pocket, drew out his pen, and wrote a check for the full amount. Davis was stunned and evidently disappointed, but who could balk at a $760 million profit?

Of course, in addition to the Pebble Beach Golf Links, Isutani had bought the Spyglass Hill, Spanish Bay and Del Monte golf courses, the Lodge at Pebble Beach and the Inn at Spanish Bay, and 17-Mile Drive, the scenic road that winds through the Del Monte Forest past its lavishly expensive houses. Soon, though, the new owner wondered if it was worth it, for Isutani lived through a rocky stewardship.

First, Monterey County raised the property's assessment for tax purposes from $220 million to $860 million, then it turned down his plan to form the Pebble Beach National Golf Club and sell 1,500 memberships for $150,000 each, enabling members to reserve starting times five years in advance. After months of hearings and threatened lawsuits, the California Coastal Commission rejected the plan because the Commission insisted on public access to the courses.

With the Japanese economy going badly and Isutani facing a financial crisis, by January 1992, he had had enough. He sold the property to Lone Cypress, a company owned by Taiheiyo Club Inc., another Japanese group that owned resorts. When Lone Cypress took over, its spokesman announced it would act as a steward until a U.S. group would take over.

Then, in June 1999, Lone Cypress announced it had sold Pebble Beach to a consortium made up of Arnold Palmer, Clint Eastwood, Richard Ferris, Peter Ueberroth and a number of other investors.

The selling price was given as $820 million. Considering how much Morse paid for it, he would have been pleased.

16

100th U.S. Open

The 18th hole, par 5 and 543 yards.

Jack Nicklaus had played in every U.S. Open since 1957, and had won four.

100th U.S. OPEN
Prologue

Late on the Friday afternoon of the U.S. Open, Jack Nicklaus stepped onto the 18th tee at Pebble Beach. Wearing a tight-lipped smile, he waved his cap at the gallery, then drove his ball into prime position in the fairway, past the two sentinel pine trees to the right, long enough to leave him roughly 240 yards from the green.

Savoring the moment, Jack whipped his 3-wood from his bag, poured everything he had into his next shot, and ripped it onto the green. The huge crowd, massed to watch him finish, roared as the ball hit precisely onto the chute between the two guarding bunkers and skipped onto the front. Grinning broadly now, Nicklaus waved to the crowd, and with his son Jackie lugging his bag, his wife, Barbara, and his other sons walking along the ropes, strode ahead to finish the last hole he would ever play in this championship. He had decided that, at the age of 60, he'd had enough.

It was an inspiring finishing touch, like Ted Williams hitting a home run his last time at bat in Fenway Park. In four previous Opens at Pebble Beach, Nicklaus hadn't once tried to reach that green with his second shot. When he won in 1972, he had played the 18th so cautiously he bogeyed. But then he had led by four strokes, so he still won easily over Bruce Crampton.

That had been 28 years ago. There was no championship at stake here; even if he had holed his second shot he wouldn't have survived the 36-hole cut. He stood 11 strokes over par for the round and needed a par 5 to shoot 82.

His eyes clouded by tears — either from the wind, as he insisted, or from emotion, as everyone hoped — Nicklaus three-putted and made his 5.

Untraditionally, the man who had made every important putt he had ever looked at left his first two putts short, his first by 10 feet and his second by less than an inch. He had his 5 and his 82, and the Open had seen the last of an enduring hero.

Again the grandstands erupted with applause for this gallant old warrior who had meant so much to the Open. Meantime, back up the fairway, waiting to play his approach, Tom Watson, Nicklaus' great rival of the 1970s and 1980s, laid down his club and clapped his hands. David Gossett, the U.S. Amateur champion, and Don Pooley, who had played with Nicklaus, rushed to shake his hand, and Jackie threw his arms around his father. Then they walked off together to meet Barbara and the rest of the family.

Nicklaus had had a long and rewarding Open career. He had begun as a 17-year-old prodigy in 1957, and he had played in every Open since, a string of 44 years. No one else had played in nearly so many.

Over that lifetime, Nicklaus had won four championships — in 1962, 1967, 1972 and 1980. No one had won more, and only Willie Anderson, Bob Jones and Ben Hogan had won as many.

Nicklaus' Open record goes beyond those he won, though. He had placed second in four, third in one, fourth in two others and from sixth through 10th in seven more.

It is always fun, though, to compare the great players of different eras. Anderson ran up his record just as the 19th century ended and the 20th began, so long ago it is impossible to judge, but Jones and Hogan left lasting records we can examine.

Jones placed second in four as well, two of

Prologue

Tiger Woods had won at Pebble Beach earlier in 2000.

those playoff losses. In a career that spanned only 11 Opens, Jones finished fifth, eighth and 11th in the others.

Although he crammed his four Open championships into six years, Hogan posed a constant threat from 1940, when he placed fifth, through 1960, when he tied for ninth after gambling and losing at the last two holes at Cherry Hills in Denver. Twenty-year-old Jack Nicklaus had played 36 holes with Hogan that day. This was the Open Arnold Palmer won. Nicklaus finished second for the first time.

No one has matched the durability of Nicklaus. His four championships span 18 years, from his first in 1962, through his last in 1980. Two years later, only Watson's miracle shot at Pebble Beach's 17th hole kept him from a fifth Open, and the following year he placed second in the PGA Championship. Four years later, when he was 46, he won the 1986 Masters — a period of 27 seasons when he was playing well enough to have won any of the game's most important competitions.

No one has meant more to championship golf. For so many years he was a constant threat and a constant thrill to watch. The longest straight driver the game had known, he hit as many greens as any of the great players. When he won the 1967 Open, he hit 61 greens at Baltusrol, a phenomenal record.

It was there that week that he ended the reign of Palmer, although Arnold remained a dangerous rival for several years. Then Nicklaus fought off challenges from first Lee Trevino and later Watson, and outlasted both.

Was he the greatest golfer of them all? Many close followers of the game believe he was, and his 18 major championships are a powerful argument for him.

Some say we'll never see his like again. Perhaps, but during his final march up an 18th fairway of an Open, some others pointed to the practice putting green, where Tiger Woods was preparing to carve his own historic tale.

Just 24 years old, Woods had already become the best player in the game — by any measurement. As the Open week began, he had won 19 PGA Tour events, and 25 around the world, in little more than 3½ years as a professional. He had won

100th U.S. Open

A memorial service was held for Payne Stewart, the 1999 champion who died in an airplane accident.

four earlier in 2000, most spectacularly the Pebble Beach National Pro-Am in February, when he stood seven strokes out of the lead with seven holes to play. Never out of contention so long as there are holes to play, Woods caught and passed PGA Tour rookie Matt Gogel by closing with 64 while Gogel stumbled through the last nine holes in 40. Woods sparked his rally by holing a 95-yard pitch for an eagle 2 at the 15th, then nearly holing another at the 16th, leaving his ball just three feet from the hole. He birdied.

That was the sixth consecutive PGA Tour event he had won, reaching back into 1999, the longest streak since Hogan won six in 1948. Woods had also won the Mercedes Championships in Hawaii a month before the Pebble Beach event, the Bay Hill Invitational in March and the Memorial Tournament three weeks before the Open.

There was no question Woods would go to Pebble Beach as the man to beat. He had shown he would have to be dealt with from the beginning of his professional career when he won the fifth tournament he entered, beating Davis Love III in a playoff in the 90-hole Las Vegas Invitational. He had closed with 64 after shooting an earlier round of 63.

Still, Woods wasn't invincible. In head-to-head competitions earlier in the 2000 season, Darren Clarke had beaten him by 4 and 3 in the final match of the Andersen Consulting Match Play tournament late in February, and holing the kind of putts Woods usually gobbles up, Hal Sutton had beaten him by one stroke in The Players Championship five weeks later.

A round-faced, hulking Irishman from Portrush in Northern Ireland, Clarke had been shaken awake by Colin Montgomerie a year or so earlier. As Nicklaus had once scolded Lee Trevino, Montgomerie laid into Clarke, disgusted that he had been wasting so much talent. Responding to Mont-

Prologue

Darren Clarke had beaten Woods earlier.

Hal Sutton had regained his 1980s form.

Vijay Singh held the Masters title.

gomerie's anger, Clarke began working seriously on his game, and by mid-June he led the Order of Merit on the PGA European Tour. Emphasizing how far he had come, on his way to winning the match-play event, Clarke defeated Paul Azinger, Mark O'Meara, Thomas Bjorn, Hal Sutton and David Duval, ranked second in the world, before beating Woods.

It was good to see that Sutton had broken loose from a slump that had lasted years. From the 1986 Memorial Tournament until the 1998 Texas Open, he had won only once. It seemed a shame. He had come onto the PGA Tour after an outstanding college career, climaxed by winning the U.S. Amateur in 1980. Three years later he won both the Tournament Players Championship and the PGA Championship, added four more tournaments over the next three years, then fell apart.

Weathering many off-course difficulties, Sutton found his game once again, won twice in 1998, including the Tour Championship, and once more in 1999. After winning the 2000 Players, he placed

David Duval was ranked second in the world.

100th U.S. Open

10th in the Masters, won again at Greensboro, then tied for eighth at the Memorial.

One would have thought no one would have been better poised for the Open than Vijay Singh, the man who has torn up more sod on practice grounds than any living being. After all, he had won the 1998 PGA Championship, and even more impressively, played the last 54 holes at Augusta in 206 and won the Masters in April. But after placing third the following week, Singh had played some indifferent golf, finishing no higher than 24th in the five tournaments leading up to the Open. He had had his best Open finish in 1999, tying for third with Woods at Pinehurst, just two strokes behind Payne Stewart and one behind Phil Mickelson. (On Wednesday morning of the Open week, a memorial service was held for Stewart, who died along with three associates and two pilots in an airplane accident in October.)

By winning three tournaments earlier in the year, Mickelson had won only one fewer than Woods, and off his close run at Pinehurst, he came into the Open a serious threat. He certainly seemed capable of shooting any score at all. Over the season he had shot three 63s, one 64 and two 65s. He had won the Buick Invitational with a 66-67-67 start, the 54-hole BellSouth Classic with 67-69-69 and the Colonial with a 63 finish. He had finished the Byron Nelson Classic with a 63-68-65 rush, but he only tied Jesper Parnevik and Love. Mickelson went out at the second playoff hole, and Parnevik beat Love at the third.

This was Parnevik's second victory of the year. Earlier he had won the 90-hole Bob Hope Classic with five rounds in the 60s, the last two 64 and 65. Furthermore, he had proved himself as a big-event player, especially in the British Open, where he had been a perpetual threat ever since he nearly won the 1994 championship at Turnberry.

He had played in only three U.S. Opens, though, and had placed in the top 20 the last two times out. An eccentric dresser, sometimes wearing flaming colors and at other times dull black, Parnevik sometimes swallows volcanic dust to clear out his insides. Rubbing some on his clubs might help him more, because clothes don't necessarily make the man at Pebble Beach.

Phil Mickelson was a threat, with three victories.

Jesper Parnevik was another proven winner.

The first group — Mark Brooks, Brent Geiberger and Bob May — was off at 6:30.

100th U.S. OPEN
First Round

The first day of the 100th U.S. Open was unlike any first day at the other 99.

It began with Hal Sutton holing a soft 8-iron shot for an eagle 2 at the first hole and ended with about half the field stumbling around in the gloom wondering where the course had gone.

In between:
- Flashing some of his old brilliance, Nick Faldo sprang to life and played the first 11 holes in four under par.
- Even more unexpected, Bobby Clampett, a prodigy of the early 1980s, left his television duties and came out of hibernation with an opening 68.
- Pebble Beach's new fifth hole revealed itself as a brutally hard par 3.
- Without a defending champion, since Payne Stewart had died in an airplane accident, the U.S. Open also lost the British Open champion when Paul Lawrie withdrew.
- And, living up to most predictions, Tiger Woods raced to the front by shooting 65, beating the lowest score ever shot in three previous Opens at Pebble Beach.

It had been quite a day. It opened in crisp and cool weather, but by mid-morning a sea mist had drifted in, clouding the view of fairway and green, then thinned and moved on. The warning was ominous. Ron Read, who starts the U.S. Open field, lived in Carmel Valley and knew what might happen. He warned that at this time of the year, the fog becomes so thick that play has to be canceled occasionally. But that lay ahead.

Meantime, under clear skies and only a light offshore breeze, Pebble Beach seemed vulnerable. Besides Sutton, John Huston, in the second group off the tee, went out in 33 and shot 67, and Spaniard Miguel Angel Jimenez scored even better, playing the first seven holes in five under par and shooting 66.

Meanwhile, some of the older players were doing extremely well, too. Fifty-five-year-old Hale Irwin, who had won his third Open a decade earlier, shot 68. Tom Kite, who had won the 1992 Open at Pebble Beach, shot 72. As for the other Pebble Beach Open champions, Tom Watson (1982) shot 71, and Jack Nicklaus (1972) shot 73.

Vijay Singh, the 2000 Masters winner, shot 70; Phil Mickelson, runner-up to Stewart a year earlier, shot 71, and Loren Roberts, who had come so close in 1994 but lost to Ernie Els, was among the three who shot 68.

Among those who didn't play nearly so well, David Duval, second in the World Ranking, fell to 75, along with Davis Love III. Further back, both Nick Price and Greg Norman shot 77s.

Scoring in general was pretty good. Ten men shot in the 60s, seven others shot 70, and 11 matched Pebble Beach's par of 71, for a total of 28 rounds of par or better. The figures compared almost exactly with the opening round of 1992, when 29 men were at 71, that year one under.

For a time Sutton looked as if he might run away from the field. As an encore to his eagle at the first hole, the first eagle at the opening hole since Deane Beman holed a 4-wood at Baltusrol in 1967, Sutton birdied the second with a 5-iron to three feet from 196 yards, went to the turn in 31, birdied the 12th and 13th to go six under par, then fell apart.

Overshooting the 14th, the long, uphill par 5, he chipped back over the green with his fourth

25

First Round

John Huston (67) birdied the first and third.

Miguel Angel Jimenez (66) was five under par.

Bobby Clampett (68) was a hometown favorite.

First Round

Tiger Woods	65	-6
Miguel Angel Jimenez	66	-5
John Huston	67	-4
Bobby Clampett	68	-3
Hale Irwin	68	-3
Loren Roberts	68	-3
Hal Sutton	69	-2
Angel Cabrera	69	-2
Rocco Mediate	69	-2
Nick Faldo	69	-2

shot, chipped again, then two-putted for a double-bogey 7. Four under par now, he struggled the rest of the way, bogeying the 16th and the 18th. His Open bid had ended.

As Sutton, Lee Westwood and Steve Jones reached the home hole, the fog was closing in. They aimed their drives at the pine trees, their only visible target. The green, 543 yards away, was hidden in the mist. Judging distance was guesswork; every shot was risky. Sailboats bobbing in gentle swells faded into the haze like ghost ships from a Wagnerian opera.

There were further problems. By then the fifth hole had turned into a bottleneck. It played so hard and took so long, five groups had backed up on the tee by noon. Rick Hartmann, a club professional from Bridgehampton, New York, played his tee shot at 11:40, then waited 15 minutes before stroking his first putt. At 12:20 the USGA interrupted the start of play, setting all times back half an hour. The 12:20 group of Lee Janzen, Ernie Els and Bob Estes would start instead at 12:50. Now it seemed certain the entire field couldn't complete the first round.

Both Huston and Jimenez would, though, since they had begun in early morning. Starting at 6:40 Thursday, Huston played three holes before making a par. He birdied the first and third, holing putts of 10 and 12 feet, bogeyed the second, then birdied both the sixth, the par 5, and the seventh, holing from 12 and 20 feet. Another bogey at the eighth and he had gone out in 33.

With another birdie at the 10th, where he holed from 35 feet, and still another at the 11th from 25 feet, he finished at four under par.

Even with his 67, there was some question of Huston's staying power, since the Open is not one of his specialties. He had played in nine Opens, missed the cut in five of the first six, and in his last three had tied for 82nd, 32nd and 17th. He had been improving.

So had Jimenez, although not markedly. He had been in only two Opens, at Shinnecock Hills in 1995 and Pinehurst in 1999, tying for 28th and 23rd. Earlier in 2000 he had done little in the

Loren Roberts (68) had six birdies.

Hale Irwin (68) was the low senior.

United States, and in five events on the PGA European Tour he had finished no higher than a tie for sixth in Germany.

Nevertheless, he surprised everyone with his marvelous putting. He one-putted nine greens, six

First Round

Rocco Mediate (69) birdied the ninth and 10th holes.

Nick Faldo (69) dropped two strokes on the last five holes.

Hal Sutton (69) was six under when he double-bogeyed the 14th.

Angel Cabrera (69) birdied two of the last three holes.

of them for birdies, and chipped in for another at the second hole. He holed his longest putt from 30 feet at the seventh and his shortest from two inches to save his par at the eighth. Jimenez closed with a fine bunker shot at the 18th, then holed the birdie putt.

Through much of his round, Jimenez had been chasing Woods, who had begun early enough to avoid the worst of the weather and the worst of the hold-up at the fifth hole.

Everyone had been waiting for Tiger. Crowds lined every fairway four and five deep, sometimes deeper around the greens, and he didn't disappoint them.

Woods played one of those rounds that could have been lots worse. While he shaved par by six strokes, he saved himself from some loose iron play with remarkable poise and exquisite touch on the greens. Six times he salvaged pars either from off the green or after a poor first putt. At the ninth hole, for example, he ran a bold putt eight feet past, but turned around and holed it coming back. He saved two other pars from 12 feet on both the

100th U.S. Open

Tiger Woods (65) had 12 one-putt greens in the first round.

First Round

Tom Kite (72) started with three bogeys.

11th and 17th holes, and another from six feet at the 15th. All of them could have been missed.

Certainly he had played a few off-color irons, but others had rattled the flagstick — a sand wedge to a foot at the fourth, a 9-iron to a foot at the 13th, another pitch to one foot at the 14th and a bunker shot to a foot and a half at the 18th.

He hit 11 of the 14 fairways on driving holes, which is pretty good, considering how far he hits the ball, and he hit 12 greens.

His putting touch had rescued his round. He had been disappointed with his work on the greens when he arrived at Pebble Beach, so he spent two hours or so on Wednesday working on his posture and the position of his hands. The changes worked marvels. He one-putted 12 greens in that first round, had 24 putts in all, and he hadn't three-putted once. What he had done, though, was establish himself as the first-round leader, and when he is in front, he's very difficult to beat.

Meantime, Darren Clarke, Fred Couples and Jeff Maggert had left the first tee at 1 o'clock, following the delayed starting times. When they reached the 10th tee, the last of that seven-hole run along the coastline, the fog had closed in. Claiming he couldn't see well enough to drive,

Phil Mickelson (71) played through the mid-day fog.

100th U.S. Open

Maggert called for a rules official.

Tom Meeks, the USGA's Director of Rules and Competitions, rushed to the spot and agreed with Maggert. Play was suspended. It was 3:57. Only a little more than half the field had finished, another 75 were still on the course, and the last group stood on the third tee.

The players were told to hold their positions because the fog might clear, but meantime, some chipped and putted to holes they had already finished, others giggled trying to balance three balls atop one another on a peg tee, or else they simply waited.

On the fifth tee, a couple of European caddies talked of fog delays at Monte Carlo, on cliffs above the Mediterranean. "When the fog comes in there," one laughed, "you'd better not wander off or you might step off the edge."

Nearly 2½ hours passed, then play was called off for the day. It was 6:28. Those with holes to play were to start again at 6:30 Friday morning, finish their first round, then tee off for their second round.

The delay caught Faldo on the 14th tee still four under par, grouped with Kirk Triplett and Corey Pavin at three under. Loren Roberts was three under after seven holes, Hale Irwin two under, Tom Watson one under, Fred Couples even, and Tom Kite, Darren Clarke and Jack Nicklaus two over after nine. Ernie Els was one under after 10 holes, and Colin Montgomerie, Vijay Singh and Greg Norman were even par after seven.

It didn't affect John Daly, though. Having another of his seizures as he played the 18th hole, Daly drove one ball out of bounds, pounded three more shots into the ocean, took a drop in a bunker, used two more to get out, made 14, shot 83, and walked off into the sunset. He wouldn't be back for the second round.

With a fresh offshore wind the USGA's plan might have worked and the second round could have finished Friday afternoon, but when those with holes to play arrived at Pebble Beach, some after getting up at 4 o'clock in the morning, the coast still lay under a foggy blanket. The starting times were pushed back to 8:15. Now it was a rush to see how many could finish the second round.

The delay obviously had its effect. His momentum stopped, Faldo bogeyed the 14th, double-bogeyed the 17th, and saved a 69 with a birdie at the 18th. Roberts held on to what he had and finished with 68, but Triplett lost two strokes and finished with 70. Pavin did worse, dropping four strokes over the last five holes for 72, his round ruined by a 7 at the 14th.

Nicklaus, out in 37, played a strong second nine, shot 36 coming in, and finished the round with 73, a good score, but he still had 18 more holes to play. On what was to be his last day of Open competition, Nicklaus would have to play 27 holes.

It seemed a lot to ask of the usual 60-year-old man, but who considered Nicklaus usual?

Tom Watson (71) had a solid start.

Sergio Garcia (75) posted one birdie.

Colin Montgomerie (73) double-bogeyed the par-5 14th hole.

Tiger Woods (134) showed his intensity as he followed this tee shot.

100th U.S. OPEN
Second Round

A persistent morning fog and brisk afternoon winds raised the suspicion that the 100th Open might last another century. Once again the complete field didn't finish the scheduled round, but then there had been little chance it would. And while Tiger Woods continued to play as everyone knew he could, no one else made a move.

Because of the mist, the field couldn't start the day's play until 8:15, an hour and 45 minutes behind schedule, and those who had to complete their first rounds had barely time enough to gobble a sandwich before they teed off for their second. Players and caddies stuffed apples into their pockets and staged a raid on granola bars. Their sandwiches vanished in two or three gulps, and they swept up water bottles faster than hikers headed for the Mojave.

Thursday's last group — Michael Harris, Mike Troy and Jeff Lee — began from the third tee Friday morning, completed their first round at 1:27 p.m., 22½ hours after they had begun, and teed off again at 2 o'clock. Naturally the day ended with a bedraggled bunch of players still with holes to play. Nineteen groups, 57 men, were left stranded when the USGA suspended the round in semi-darkness at 8:15 Friday evening.

Woods had just birdied the 12th hole when the USGA called it a day. By then he stood nine under par for 30 holes, three ahead of Miguel Angel Jimenez, who had played 25 holes at six under. Woods stood three under for the day, Jimenez one under. Even though the next morning Woods played some shabby golf by his standards, his lead grew to six strokes when Jimenez began playing loose shots. His collapse had given Woods the largest 36-hole lead the U.S. Open had ever seen.

Thomas Bjorn, a 29-year-old Dane, and Angel Cabrera, a 30-year-old Argentinean, stood at two under par at the suspension, Bjorn after 16 holes, Cabrera after nine. When the round finally ended the next morning, Bjorn had held on and shot another 70, but Cabrera, confident after 27 holes, lost his game and went from 69 in the first round to 76 in the second.

Others suffered the same affliction as Cabrera. After opening with 67, John Huston slipped to 75, Jimenez shot up from 66 to 74, and Hal Sutton went from 69 to 73.

Even though Jimenez and Huston lost so many strokes, they didn't lose much ground to the rest of the field. Jimenez, in fact, held onto a share of second place with Bjorn at 140; Kirk Triplett and Jose Maria Olazabal followed at 141. Huston, Sutton and Lee Westwood tied for sixth at 142.

Few players improved their scoring, but by the end of the championship on Sunday, only two of them mattered. Irishman Padraig Harrington improved two strokes, from 73 to 71, climbing from a tie for 39th into a tie for 11th, and Ernie Els cut one stroke from his opening score by shooting 73, jumping from a tie for 53rd to a tie for 36th. It didn't take much to gain ground.

Dave Eichelberger made the most impressive recovery, paring nine strokes off his opening 78 by shooting 69, and both Woody Austin and Nick Price picked up seven strokes, from 77 to 70. They didn't matter; they were too far behind in a tie for 36th.

Others went the other way. Bobby Clampett, who surprised everyone with his opening 68,

Second Round

Second Round

Tiger Woods	65 - 69 – 134	-8
Thomas Bjorn	70 - 70 – 140	-2
Miguel Angel Jimenez	66 - 74 – 140	-2
Kirk Triplett	70 - 71 – 141	-1
Jose Maria Olazabal	70 - 71 – 141	-1
John Huston	67 - 75 – 142	E
Hal Sutton	69 - 73 – 142	E
Lee Westwood	71 - 71 – 142	E
Nick Faldo	69 - 74 – 143	+1
Vijay Singh	70 - 73 – 143	+1

slipped to 77, and both Hale Irwin and Loren Roberts played worse. Both men had opened with 68s and lost 10 strokes in the second round, each shooting 78.

While most players appeared to be stumbling along, either losing strokes by the fistful or gaining a few, Woods was shooting another sub-par score, one of only seven during the round. Only 69s by Eichelberger and Joe Daley matched his. When Woods finished Saturday morning he had

Thomas Bjorn (140) went out in 32.

Kirk Triplett (141) shot 71 despite two double bogeys.

Jose Maria Olazabal (141) birdied two of the last three.

scored 134 for the first 36 holes, tying the record Jack Nicklaus had set at Baltusrol in 1980, and that Tze-Chung Chen had equaled at Oakland Hills in 1985 and Lee Janzen matched at Baltusrol in 1993.

More important to him, he had opened a six-stroke gap between himself and Jimenez and Bjorn, one stroke better than Mike Souchak's five-stroke lead at Cherry Hills in 1960. That was the year when Arnold Palmer stormed from seven strokes behind in the last round and won the championship. There would be no surge this time; there was no Arnold Palmer in the pack chasing Woods.

There would be no Jack Nicklaus, either. Perhaps drained from playing nine holes in the morning, Nicklaus had nothing further to give in the afternoon. With two double bogeys on the first nine holes, one of them at the fifth, his own design, and only four pars on the second nine, he shot 41-41–82. He finished with style, though. Resting on the rail fence behind the 18th tee, he said to his son Jackie, who caddied for him, "I haven't tried to knock it on this green in over 20 years. Let's see if I can."

He usually drove with a 3-wood, but he played

Miguel Angel Jimenez (140) fell Saturday morning.

John Huston (142) had 75, including 7 at the second.

Second Round

Bobby Clampett (145) had 77 to fall 11 strokes back.

Jack Nicklaus (155) bowed out with his son and caddie, Jackie, embracing on the 18th.

Vijay Singh (143) shot 73 with three bogeys.

his driver, then the 3-wood and made it to the green. With the par 5 he shot 155, six strokes over the cut, which fell at 149.

Greg Norman, hobbling with a painful hip, shot 159, with 82 in the second round. Jesper Parnevik went out with 153, along with amateurs David Gossett, the U.S. Amateur champion, and Aaron Baddeley, the Australian Open champion. Davis Love III and Bernhard Langer missed the cut as well. Curtis Strange, the last man to win consecutive Opens, in 1988 and 1989, couldn't break 80 in either round, and Shigeki Maruyama, the Japanese golfer who stunned everyone with a 58 in a qualifying round near Washington, D.C., shot 77-80–157.

Harassed again by a rude spectator, Colin Montgomerie, Europe's best golfer, survived nevertheless with indifferent scores of 73 and 74, and 20-year-old Spaniard Sergio Garcia, who had made such an impression in the 1999 PGA Championship, came back from an opening 75 and shot 71 in the second round.

Surviving wasn't much help, though, because Woods was obviously outplaying everybody, even though he wasn't as sharp as he had been for the first round. His driving wasn't as effective; where he had hit 11 fairways his first time around, he hit only eight the second, and only two of those Saturday morning. Still, he managed to hit 12 greens, as many as he had in the first round; he still hadn't three-putted, and once again he holed some key putts to save pars.

Woods had started at 4:40 Friday afternoon with a routine par 4 at the first hole, and then he

100th U.S. Open

Woods, with caddie Steve Williams, hit 12 greens in each of the first two rounds.

Second Round

Hal Sutton (142) took double bogey at the 16th.

Lee Janzen (144).

Lee Westwood (142).

Tom Lehman (144) bogeyed the last two holes for 73.

ran into his first lapse. His approach to the second skipped into a bunker, and after he played what he called a great bunker shot, he holed from 15 feet for the par, the kind of putt he had holed all day Thursday.

He admitted later that that putt might have been a turning point, even though it fell so early in the round. Speaking of it later he said, "I knew I had to bury that putt to get some positive momentum going."

The momentum indeed going, he rolled in another putt from 30 feet at the third hole, birdied two more on the first nine, but then offset them with two bogeys. He went out in 34, one under par.

After another routine par 4 at the 10th, his approach to the 11th took a good bounce and pulled up three feet from the hole. The putt fell.

Phil Mickelson (144) didn't challenge as expected.

Davis Love III (154) went out with 75 and 79.    *Jesper Parnevik (153) shot 80 to miss the 36-hole cut.*

He was two under for the round. He tried to nurse a long putt close, and it dropped into the hole at the 12th for another birdie. Three under par.

Now, in failing light, the day's play ended. Woods would be back to finish at 6:30 Saturday morning.

The overnight delay seemed to affect him as badly as everyone else. Of the 12 holes he had played before the break, he had hit six fairways and nine greens. When he returned Saturday morning, he hit only two of the remaining five fairways and three of the six greens, and bogeyed the 14h and 18th, both par-5 holes, the kind he birdies as often as he pars. He could figure he lost at least two strokes to the field on those two holes. Actually, he lost a little more than strokes. When he yanked his drive into the ocean alongside the 18th, he melted the television cables with a burst of foul language that would have scorched the hide of a rhinoceros. Unfortunately for everyone, television's ubiquitous parabolic microphones picked up every syllable and beamed it from San Francisco to Zanzibar.

It didn't seem to bother Woods; he teed up another ball and made 4. Adding the appropriate penalty, his scorecard showed 6. After the round, he apologized for the outburst.

Woods' lead had grown to record scope, but he had to keep up the pressure. Even though Jimenez had slipped further back, he was still hanging on, and now he had Bjorn and Harrington, two of the younger Europeans, moving up.

Jimenez was the more experienced, though. Thirty-six years old, he had been playing golf at its highest levels for 18 years, half his life, and although he might not have the game to battle Woods on even terms, he wasn't about to flinch. He had sparked Spain to its victory in the Alfred Dunhill Cup at St. Andrews in October 1999, and he had played on Europe's Ryder Cup team in September, losing a tough match to Steve Pate in the singles. Besides, he'd come up against Woods in the past and hadn't been intimidated.

He had stumbled finishing his second round Saturday morning, which wasn't a good sign. One under for the day and six under for 25 holes when he had to quit Friday, he missed six consecutive greens and bogeyed the eighth, 10th, 11th and 12th holes.

Jimenez righted his listing ship for a time, running off four consecutive pars, but he missed the 17th green and bogeyed, then helped himself with a closing birdie at the 18th. With 39 on the homeward nine, Jimenez fell so far behind Woods he would need a great third round to recover.

If not him, somebody would have to play the round of his life or the Open would become a romp.

Tiger Woods (205) recovered from a triple bogey for 71 to lead by 10 strokes.

100th U.S. OPEN
Third Round

Miguel Angel Jimenez had a gripe. Interviewed after he shot 66 in the first round, one stroke more than Tiger Woods, Jimenez complained, "I'm a little tired of this. Yes, Tiger's the best player in the game, but do you think there's only one player here? There are 156 players here."

That was then. But after the U.S. Open's third round, this was now, and as far as anyone could see, Woods stood alone. By shooting 71, which matched Pebble Beach's par, he had opened a 10-stroke chasm between himself and the men closest behind him.

When the sun went down with the Open finally back on schedule, Woods stood eight under par, at 205. Among the 63 men left in the field, only Ernie Els broke par in the third round. Playing marvelous golf, Els shot 68 and climbed 35 places into second place. It sounds impressive, but Els had a 54-hole score of 215.

On a trying day, with the wind gusting in from the sea, the playing conditions Saturday had become so difficult, especially for the early starters, that scores considered ordinary either moved players ahead or did them little damage.

Jimenez, for example, stumbled to 76, but he dropped only one place, from second into a tie for third at 216, alongside Padraig Harrington. Phil Mickelson shot a second consecutive 73, which in other circumstances would have done little for him, yet here earned him a share of fifth place at 217 with Jose Maria Olazabal, another 76 shooter.

Thomas Bjorn, however, did pay a price. From a tie for second after 36 holes, he sank to a tie for 22nd place by shooting 82 and dropping 17 strokes off the lead. He was not alone. Fifteen others shot in the 80s.

Woods' even-par round was actually second best of the day, matched only by Michael Campbell of New Zealand, and Harrington was one of only five who shot 72.

Meantime, aside from Bjorn's collapse, Vijay Singh shot 80; Hal Sutton, playing like a weekend hacker, went out in 44 and shot 83, and Kirk Triplett, right on Woods' heels when the day began, shot 84 and landed 20 strokes behind first place. Darren Clarke, who had been leading the European money list and given a strong chance to play well here, shot 83, and Sergio Garcia shot 81.

The eighth hole had been especially unpleasant. With its carry across the gorge and its tiny green, it claimed 31 bogeys and 22 pars. Only Fred Couples birdied, and both Garcia and Colin Montgomerie scored 8s. Montgomerie shot 79.

It had been a difficult day, not only for the players but for the USGA as well. In truth, the Open had been an administrative nightmare, the kind of predicament the governing body had fretted over 35 years earlier when it abandoned the Open's traditional 36-hole closing day. Sensing that some day the Open might face the same chaotic circumstances it found at Pebble Beach, the Executive Committee voted to extend the championship to four days, eliminating the double round.

The test finally came, and the Association handled the perplexing situation fairly smoothly.

When the final strokes of the second round were played Saturday morning, the field was cut to those 63 men who had finished 36 holes in 149 strokes or better, seven over par, the highest cut since a score of 151 at Oakmont in 1983. Com-

Third Round

Third Round

Tiger Woods	65 - 69 - 71 – 205	-8
Ernie Els	74 - 73 - 68 – 215	+2
Padraig Harrington	73 - 71 - 72 – 216	+3
Miguel Angel Jimenez	66 - 74 - 76 – 216	+3
Phil Mickelson	71 - 73 - 73 – 217	+4
Jose Maria Olazabal	70 - 71 - 76 – 217	+4
Lee Westwood	71 - 71 - 76 – 218	+5
John Huston	67 - 75 - 76 – 218	+5
Michael Campbell	71 - 77 - 71 – 219	+6
Loren Roberts	68 - 78 - 73 – 219	+6
Nick Faldo	69 - 74 - 76 – 219	+6

paring it to previous qualifying scores at Pebble Beach, it was four strokes higher than in 1992, but it took 151 to play the last 36 holes in 1982 and 154 to make the cut in 1972.

With the cut at 147 in 1992, Gil Morgan had led the field with 135, just one stroke above Woods' score, and beat the cut by 12 strokes. Woods' 134, just one stroke better, beat it by 15. Morgan led Andy Dillard by three strokes, but Woods led Bjorn and Jimenez by six. They had scored two strokes worse than Dillard.

As we can see, the difference between the first two rounds in 1982 and 2000 wasn't that much, but whether what happened next reflects on the level of competition between 1992 and 2000 may take some years to judge.

All that aside, after a pause following the completion of the second round, the field was re-paired and sent out again, beginning the third round at 10:40. For the first time that week, a round ended on the same day it started. Sunday's final round would follow the normal pattern, if bad weather didn't spoil the plan yet again.

Somewhat surprisingly, since they had a reputation of not performing at their best in the U.S. Open, European golfers had done quite well through the first three rounds. Of the leading 11 men after 36 holes, five were from Europe — Jimenez, Harrington, Olazabal, Lee Westwood and Nick Faldo. Michael Campbell came from New Zealand, and Els, of course, comes from South Africa.

Miguel Angel Jimenez (216) slipped to 76 and trailed Woods by 11 strokes.

Phil Mickelson (217) shot 73 while advancing from a tie for 11th to a tie for fifth place.

Other than Woods, the only Americans among them were Mickelson, tied with Olazabal for fifth place at 217, John Huston, tied with Westwood at 218, and Loren Roberts, tied for ninth with Campbell and Faldo at 219.

As the third round opened, though, three other Americans had still been in the hunt. Triplett stood seven strokes behind and Huston and Sutton eight back. Of those three only Huston played a reasonable round, while Sutton and Triplett fell like stones.

On a day when Woods played no better than par golf, only Els made a move, and that accomplished no more than move Els within 10 strokes of Woods. It did show, however, that someone other than Woods could play the course.

From his position in a tie for 35th place, Els started just before 12:30, paired with Montgomerie. After saving his par at the second hole with a good chip and putt, Els came to the fourth hole five over par, 13 strokes behind Woods. Facing Pebble Beach's shortest par-4 hole, at 331 yards,

Padraig Harrington (216) shot 72 to share third place.

Third Round

Lee Westwood (218) had 76, but tied for seventh.

Els drove with his 2-iron, then played a sand wedge for his second shot. It hit the green, bounced twice, then disappeared into the hole. An eagle 2. As he said later, "That was the kickstart I needed."

Another birdie at the sixth and he was down to two over par, 10 strokes off Woods' lead. But quickly he gave two strokes back. With the wind at his back, he overshot the little seventh green, and his 8-iron approach bounced over the eighth green, costing two strokes.

Montgomerie, meanwhile, had been playing one par after another, but after his 8, he turned in 41, double-bogeyed the 10th, birdied the 15th and stumbled home in 38. With 79 he went to 13 over par for 54 holes, 23 strokes behind Woods. It seemed a shame. Montgomerie had been a marvelous player, and he had come close in three Opens, losing twice to Els, first in a 1994 playoff, then when he bogeyed the 71st hole in 1997.

Els wasn't through just yet. He eased past the ninth hole solidly enough with a two-putt par, then, heading directly into the wind, rifled a drive

Ernie Els (215) took second place with 68.

100th U.S. Open

Jose Maria Olazabal (217) was another 76 shooter.

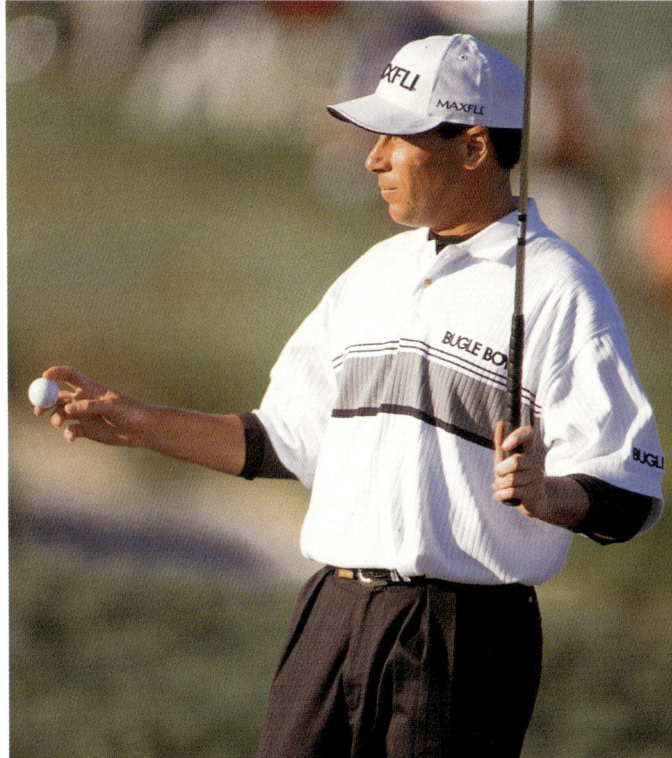

John Huston (218) claimed a birdie at the 17th.

Michael Campbell (219) shot 71 to climb from 45th.

and a full 2-iron to a green he usually reaches with a 9-iron. His ball fell short; a chip and putt and he had another par. He had played that wicked stretch of three holes in one over.

From there in he parred only half the holes, birdied three and bogeyed one. Back in 34, he had his 68.

Later Els called it one of the better rounds he had played in major championship golf, and added, "I've got half a chance."

Woods had teed off at 3:19, just behind Jimenez and Triplett, who in turn were playing behind Olazabal and Huston. Six strokes ahead when the round began, Woods birdied the second hole, opening his lead over Jimenez to eight strokes, over

45

Third Round

Kirk Triplett (225) had 84.

Hal Sutton (225) shot 83.

Vijay Singh (223) posted 80.

Thomas Bjorn (222) shot 82 and went from a second-place tie to a tie for 22nd.

Bjorn and Triplett to nine, and over Huston and Olazabal to 11.

No one had seen anything like it, but just as quickly as he opened this yawning gap, he stumbled. Playing the third hole, his second shot became entangled in heavy grass by the green. He took two strokes to chop it out, and he made 7, a triple bogey. From nine under par, he fell back to six.

As soon as the red number on the scoreboard changed from 9 to 6, the crowds gasped, perhaps wondering if Woods' lapse might inspire someone to challenge him. Now was certainly the time.

It didn't happen. As quickly as he blundered, Woods recovered, birdied three of the next six holes including a stunning punch shot on the sixth, bogeyed the eighth, where he narrowly missed that tiny green, and went out in 35, even par. Jimenez, meanwhile, played the first nine in 38, falling nine strokes behind. Both Olazabal and Triplett had fallen 10 strokes back, and Bjorn trailed by 11.

Woods played the last nine holes in even-par 36, hitting all but the 18th fairway, but he missed four greens. No matter, he one-putted each of them, three for pars. He had one escapade at the 10th, where his approach settled in front of a rock

100th U.S. Open

Woods made 7 at the par-4 third hole as he took two strokes to chop out his golf ball from the heavy grass.

With one foot in the bunker at the sixth, Tiger still maneuvered the ball 64 yards, to within birdie range.

Third Round

As Woods stood in the 10th fairway, even par for the day, his lead had grown to nine strokes.

100th U.S. Open

A birdie at the 14th was Tiger's last of the day.

in a hazard. Playing stone and all, he hurt his hand slightly chopping his ball out and bogeyed. A birdie at the 14th won that stroke back, and he finished with four pars.

There was no question that Woods had the best of the weather. Els had played through blustery winds, but as the hours passed the wind moderated, especially on the inward holes, where the fairways are protected from the full force of an ocean breeze.

Some suggested that this worked to Woods' advantage and hurt others. Perhaps, but those closest to him after 36 holes played through the same conditions, and not one of them gained ground. Of those who had played the first two rounds in par or better, he beat Olazabal, Jimenez, Huston and Westwood by five strokes, Hal Sutton by 12, and Kirk Triplett by 13.

It wasn't the weather. Those who were there were watching something very special.

Woods saved par from a bunker at the 17th to maintain his even-par round, a score beaten by just one player.

49

Tiger Woods (272), with caddie Steve Williams, completed his historic march at Pebble Beach.

100th U.S. OPEN
Fourth Round

When the great racehorse Citation trotted from the paddock for the Pimlico Special back in 1948, he had no horse to run against. Instead, it was a walkover; the starter waved his flag and Citation took a leisurely gallop around the track.

The last round of the U.S. Open felt something like that, except Tiger Woods, in Citation's role, didn't play a leisurely round of golf. He acted more like Secretariat pounding down the stretch so far ahead of the pack he won the 1973 Belmont Stakes by 31 lengths.

If we apply these racing parallels to golf, they approximate Woods in the 100th Open. He shot 67 in the last round, the best score of the day, finished at 272, and ruled the championship so thoroughly he won by 15 strokes.

Everyone else played only bit parts. Both Ernie Els and Miguel Angel Jimenez shot 287, which would have been close in two of the previous Opens at Pebble Beach and would have won the first, in 1972. John Huston took fourth place at 288; Padraig Harrington and Lee Westwood tied for fifth at 289, and Nick Faldo placed seventh at 290.

Only 10 players were beaten by fewer than 20 strokes. The others, at 291, were the Masters champion, Vijay Singh; the second-ranked player in the world, David Duval; Stewart Cink and Loren Roberts. They couldn't help feeling embarrassed by the scope of the drubbing they had taken.

The scale of Woods' dominance reached beyond understanding. These were not weekend hackers, for heaven's sake. Els had already won two U.S. Opens, and Faldo had won three Masters Tournaments and three British Opens. But as Els said as he slumped into a chair, "Is it embarrassing? It's kind of tough to take, you know. When you have the best player in the world on his game, you can't make many mistakes. You've got to play out of your mind.

"So what do we have to do to get to him? Take everything you can get and hope for the best."

Woods simply overpowered the field as he set four records and tied two others.

His records:
- Shot 65 in the first round, the lowest score in an Open at Pebble Beach.
- Played the first 36 holes in 134, tying the record held by Jack Nicklaus (1980), Tze-Chung Chen (1985) and Lee Janzen (1993).
- Led by six strokes after 36 holes, breaking the record of five strokes held by Willie Anderson since 1903 and matched by Mike Souchak in 1960.
- Led by 10 strokes after 54 holes, breaking the record of seven strokes held by Jim Barnes since 1921.
- Shot 272, tying the 72-hole record held by Jack Nicklaus since 1980 and matched by Lee Janzen in 1993.
- His 15-stroke margin over the runners-up broke the record of 11 strokes Willie Smith had set in 1899.

Additionally, he not only led every round, he built on his lead every day, from one stroke after the first, to six after the second, to 10 after the third and finally to 15 at the end.

Woods' accomplishment exceeded any performance you can think of. Willie Smith's record had been set so long ago under such different conditions — like the gutta-percha ball and hickory-shafted clubs — it doesn't relate to modern times.

Fourth Round

Miguel Angel Jimenez (287) tied for second, but felt he "played a different championship."

Padraig Harrington (289) was among the four Europeans in the top seven finishers.

100th U.S. Open

Fourth Round

Tiger Woods	65 - 69 - 71 - 67 – 272	-12
Miguel Angel Jimenez	66 - 74 - 76 - 71 – 287	+3
Ernie Els	74 - 73 - 68 - 72 – 287	+3
John Huston	67 - 75 - 76 - 70 – 288	+4
Lee Westwood	71 - 71 - 76 - 71 – 289	+5
Padraig Harrington	73 - 71 - 72 - 73 – 289	+5
Nick Faldo	69 - 74 - 76 - 71 – 290	+6
Vijay Singh	70 - 73 - 80 - 68 – 291	+7
Stewart Cink	77 - 72 - 72 - 70 – 291	+7
David Duval	75 - 71 - 74 - 71 – 291	+7
Loren Roberts	68 - 78 - 73 - 72 – 291	+7

Comparison is useless.

It is the same with Old Tom Morris in the 1862 British Open. Old Tom won by 13 strokes at Prestwick only months after the shooting began in the American Civil War. Morris and his cronies played only 36 holes, and the only available record shows that he beat just seven other players.

Forget all that. What we saw at Pebble Beach was unique. Never in modern times has one man so completely, thoroughly and ruthlessly destroyed

John Huston (288) shot 70 for fourth place.

Ernie Els (287) posted 72 for a share of second.

Fourth Round

the competition. He outplayed everybody. He drove the ball farther (his drive at the ninth in the last round flew 329 yards), he hit the most greens, hit his irons closer to the hole, and he holed an uncanny number of putts from 10 to 20 feet.

As Els said, "What can you do when a guy drives it 300 yards and plays 9-irons into these greens?"

On the two driving holes statisticians measured through the week, he averaged 299 yards, the best in the field. Duval came in second at 293 yards.

By hitting 41 of the 56 fairways on driving holes, he averaged 73 percent, 14th best. Naturally, Colin Montgomerie did best, hitting 46, or 82 percent. (Told he ranked first at hitting fairways, Montgomerie said, "Great. They should put the hole in the fairway.")

Woods hit 51 greens, again the best of the field. (Nicklaus, though, had hit 61 when he won at Baltusrol in 1967.)

Although he seemed to hole every putt he looked at, he tied Mark O'Meara and Huston for sixth place. Faldo outputted him, 104 to 110. Not much difference.

Lee Westwood (289) was even par for the final day.

Loren Roberts (291) shot 72 and tied for eighth place.

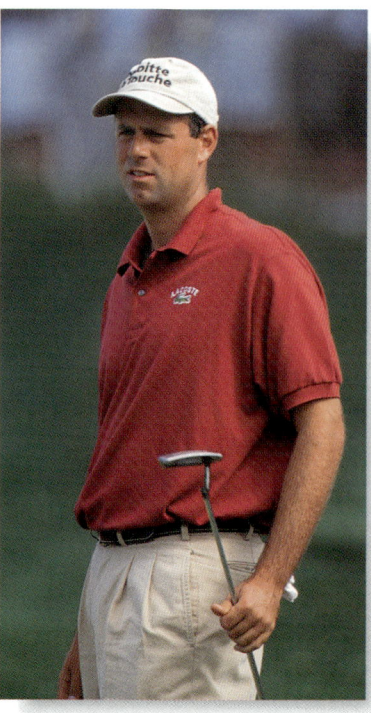

Stewart Cink (291) closed with 70 to advance into the top 10.

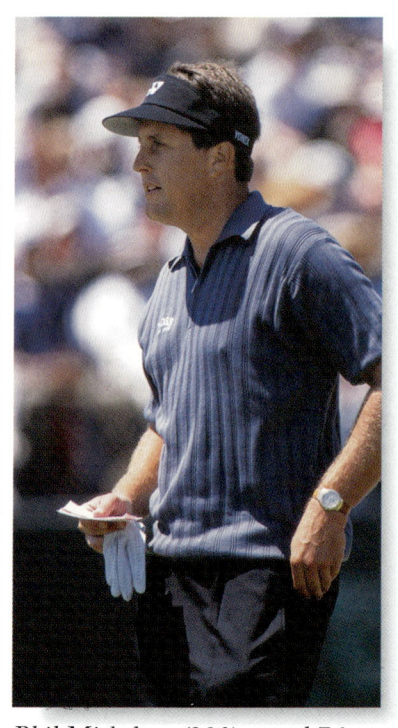

Phil Mickelson (293) posted 76 and fell to a tie for 16th.

100th U.S. Open

With this pitching wedge to the ninth, Woods completed the first nine in even par and led by nine strokes.

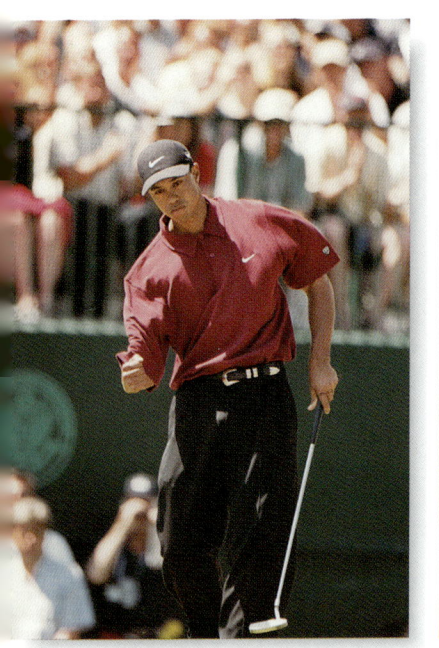

Fourth Round

An 18-foot putt at the 12th was one of Woods' four birdies over five holes to start the final nine.

Over four rounds played through the game's most intense pressure over a severe course, Woods did not three-putt a green. At the other extreme, he one-putted 34, nearly half the holes. Three times he one-putted the second, seventh, 10th, 12th, 16th and 17th.

Nor did he lose strokes at the same hole twice. He played the first and the last rounds without a bogey, and he went over par on only six holes, including his triple bogey.

Over the four rounds he birdied 21 holes, 29 percent. He birdied six in the first round, six more in the second, five in the third and four in the last. He did it under demanding conditions on a course with small greens, punishing rough and narrow fairways.

Throughout the week he played with serene confidence in his swing. Only toward the end did he appear to lose his tempo, slashing at tee shots at the 15th and 16th holes and pushing them into rough. Neither shot cost him anything; he was rescued by his blazing putter.

He appeared to be loose and relaxed going into the last round, as he should have been. With such an absurd lead, he certainly had nothing to fear from the field; he could only lose if his own game had corroded overnight.

Now 12 under, Tiger missed a birdie putt at the 15th.

From the beginning he played, if not cautious, then careful golf, not forcing his shots and not gambling on the greens and risking a long second putt.

Starting at the end of the field, paired with Els, he teed off just behind Jimenez and Harrington, leading both men by 11 strokes. Els trailed by 10. Both Jimenez and Harrington played quality approaches to the first hole and birdied. Now they were only 10 strokes back, tied with Els, and they had 17 holes to make up the difference.

Woods played the first four holes well within himself, keeping his ball below the hole so he could putt uphill, never pressing. Even playing controlled golf as he was, he might have opened a wider lead, but a couple of putts that might have fallen grazed the lip and slid past.

By the time he reached the fifth hole, though, he had lost two strokes of his lead. Three over par when they began, both Jimenez and Harrington had fought back to even par. Now they stood eight strokes behind with 12 holes to play.

Els had blundered by then and fallen 11 strokes back. Trying to make something happen, Els had been going boldly for birdies, making none, and leaving himself missable second putts. It cost him his first stroke at the fourth hole, where his ball caught the lip of the hole and spun away. He had had no realistic hope of catching Woods when the day began, and now he found himself sinking further behind.

Woods holed this putt at the 16th to avoid a bogey in his round.

Fourth Round

He took an erratic swing and lost another stroke at the fifth, yanking his tee shot into clumpy rough next to a bunker. Now he stood four over par, 12 strokes behind Woods, four behind Jimenez and Harrington.

Here Woods showed not only cool command of his game, but exquisite judgment of distance as well. He played a nice, safe 7-iron that hit the very front of the green, avoiding any risk of catching the rough, kicked a little right, and settled softly. His first putt pulled up three feet short, but he ran his second putt straight in. Eight strokes ahead, he had 13 holes to play.

Now he ran into trouble. After another Brobdingnagian drive down the hill at the sixth, the par 5, he ripped into a 4-iron. It flew up the slope toward the blind green, but his aim was off; his ball hung up in the tangled grass alongside a bunker. This was not an easy shot. Standing with his right foot dug into the sand and his left knee braced against the ground outside, Woods flew the ball all the way over and into the rough on the far side.

This is a hole he had birdied twice, but after popping his ball six feet past, he could conceivably lose a stroke. Foolish thought, of course, because he ran it in. Still eight under par, eight strokes ahead and 12 holes to play.

So it went. A sand wedge to the back left corner of the seventh hole, two putts from 30 feet, then a 4-iron from the eighth that left him atop the plateau perhaps 200 yards from the green. Again no problem. A high, floating 6-iron hugged the green. Two more putts, and on to the ninth.

Here he pounded that tremendous drive, lofted a 135-yard pitching wedge 20 feet from the hole, and two-putted. Even par for the first nine, he was still eight under par but now nine strokes ahead. Jimenez had bogeyed the ninth and dropped into a tie with Harrington at one over. Both men had played the first nine in 33.

Then Els came to life. A birdie at the ninth, still another at the 10th, and he had caught Harrington, who was losing strokes. Still, Els lagged 11 strokes behind Woods, who finally birdied, holing from 15 feet at the 10th.

The Open had been over long ago, of course, but then Woods pulled even further ahead. He

Tiger two-putted from 20 feet for the title.

His competitors were hopelessly out of contention long before Woods completed his parade down the 18th hole.

birdied the 12th, 13th and 14th holes with the kind of precision putting we hardly ever see. As the putts dropped his lead kept building — to 10 strokes after the 10th, 11 after the 12th, 12 after the 13th, and 13 after the 14th.

Jimenez had continued piling up the pars, clinging to second place, but finally he cracked. Bunkered approaches at both the 17th and 18th cost him strokes. Woods saved par with a 15-footer at the 16th and his lead grew — to 14 strokes after the 17th, and then to 15 when Jimenez missed his putt at the 18th.

Those two lost strokes cost him a clear claim to second place. After Els' bogey at the 12th, which dropped him to three over par, he had played every hole in par, shot 72, and caught Jimenez.

Once again Woods had outplayed every man in the field, but he wasn't alone in shooting in the 60s. Singh had wakened from the torpor of the 80 he had shot on Saturday, come back with 68, and climbed into a tie for eighth place. Paul Azinger, Mike Weir, Scott Hoch, Richard Zokol and Hale Irwin shot 69s, and Huston shot 70, along with three others. But they trailed far, far behind. Up ahead, the gallery waited to acclaim a new, young champion.

Woods' parade up the 18th was as regal as a Roman general's. Fans crammed the big grandstands alongside the last green, yelling, waving and calling his name, and hordes more lined the fairway, packed six, maybe 10, deep, straining to catch just a glimpse.

Striding toward the green, he took off his cap and saluted the gallery, his smile broadening as he drew closer.

He had played the final hole safely, driving with a 4-iron, laying up with an 8-iron, and then the final pitch.

As Woods studied his putt, the gallery sensed he wanted more. With his ball lying no more than 20 feet from the hole, he wanted a last birdie. Obviously going for it, he rolled his ball several feet past. No birdie here, but he rammed it home and claimed the national championship.

When the putt fell, the crowd broke into more wild cheering. Woods turned toward them, raised his right arm, and walked off, leaving all of us to wonder at the virtuosity we had seen.

The U.S. Open was Tiger Woods' seventh USGA Championship.

100th U.S. OPEN
The Champion

If the real Tiger Woods had been only myth and an author had written the story as a novel, a publisher would have kicked him out.

"And take the back stairway, please. We wouldn't want folks thinking we coddle crackpots."

Quite right, Tiger's biography does indeed read like *Beowulf*. Who would believe the authentic story of a toddler who had a tiny club thrust into his hands at the age of 2 and then grew up with the coordination, the talent, the drive, the commitment and the character to become not only the national champion but perhaps the best player the game had produced?

Behind his climb through pee wee competitions, through junior programs, college, amateur and finally professional golf lay the firm hand of Earl Woods, Tiger's father. Never modest about his precocious son, Earl had declared long ago that in his son Eldrick the world was about to see something special. Earl was a prophet.

He was his son's teacher, his drill-master, his confidant and above all his father. He encouraged him, and he probably pushed him, and told him all things were possible. But what are the probabilities that the son would have been born with all the critical and essential genetic qualities — the athleticism, the strength of will and the sense of purpose to fulfill a father's dream?

Watching the television account of Tiger's virtuoso performance from his home in Cypress, Calif., outside Los Angeles, Earl could only boast, "It was vintage Tiger, totally in control, totally in a win mode. I've kept saying you've only seen the tip of the iceberg, and people have said, 'Right, right.' Now they see what he can do."

Raised in California and nicknamed for a Vietnamese soldier Earl had known, Tiger Woods had already earned a reputation as a first-class golfer when he arrived at the Bay Hill Club in Orlando, Fla., for the 1991 U.S. Junior Amateur Championship. He won the qualifying medal and the championship. He was 15, the youngest champion ever. He won again the next year, and for the third time in 1993. Before Tiger, no one had won the Junior Amateur more than once.

No longer eligible for the Junior Amateur, Woods moved on and won the 1994 U.S. Amateur. At 18, he was the youngest champion ever. Then he won two more, becoming the first to win three consecutive U.S. Amateur titles. He had won six national championships in six years.

In late August 1996, still only 20, Woods joined the PGA Tour. In his fifth tournament, he won the 90-hole Las Vegas Invitational, beating Davis Love III in a playoff. Woods played his last four rounds in the 60s. He shot 63 in the second round and 64 in the fifth. Clearly, he might shoot any score at all.

A few weeks later he won again, a startling record for a rookie. He had also played consistently. After tying for 60th place in his first tournament, he finished 11th in his second, and followed by placing fifth or better in his next five, a run that included the two he won.

The victories kept piling up — five in 1997, two in 1998, nine in 1999 and another five in 2000. In less than four years as a professional, Woods had won 20 tournaments on the PGA Tour, plus six more victories in overseas and unofficial events. While he had won the 1999 PGA Championship, until he won at Pebble Beach in June, his biggest and most impressive victory had been the 1997

The Champion

Masters. Now, not only had he won both the Masters and the U.S. Open, he had won them spectacularly — the Masters by 12 strokes, the Open by 15.

Throughout his career he had played remarkably consistent golf. In 81 tournaments, he had missed the cut in only one. He shot 146 in the 1997 Bell Canadian Open and left town early.

His later record had been extraordinary. From the 1999 Memorial Tournament through the 2000 Open, Woods had won 12 of 22 PGA Tour events.

It gets better. When he stood seven strokes behind Matt Gogel with seven holes to play in the Pebble Beach National Pro-Am in February 2000, he brushed it aside with a flurry of sub-par golf and won his sixth consecutive PGA Tour tournament, the longest winning streak since Ben Hogan won six straight in 1948.

The Open, though, was Tiger's biggest prize. Looking back on the week, he claimed he never once felt he couldn't lose.

"To be honest," he said, "I never really felt unbeatable. But when I was on the greens I had this weird feeling. I felt very calm and at ease with myself. It's hard to describe." He said he felt that way both at Pebble Beach and at Augusta when he won the Masters.

"For some reason, things just flowed. When you have that feeling, no matter what you do, good or bad, it really doesn't get to you."

Analyzing his week's work, Woods said that when you finish a U.S. Open 12 strokes under par, as he had, you know you played well.

"This week I drove the ball beautifully and hit a lot of good iron shots, but if you look at every round, you'll see I made important putts for par. You have to make them in the Open. If you miss a green here or in any U.S. Open, you know you'll have to make the eight- or 10-footers for pars. If you make those, they feel better than birdies."

Of all the holes he played the last day, Woods liked to look back on the 16th, where he had hit his tee shot into the short rough, and from a flyer lie carried the shot over the green.

"One of my biggest moments of the day was when I holed that putt. I had worked so hard not to make a bogey, and now I had a 15-footer for a par."

He also underscored what might unsettle the competition.

"This is something I've said and I will continue to say. I'm going to try to get better. You're always working on things in this game, trying new equipment or trying new techniques. There's always something."

There is no question he has played better each year. If he continues to improve he'll leave us all wondering what may lie ahead.

Both Darren Clarke and Hal Sutton generated lots of praise by beating Woods head-to-head earlier in the year, Clarke in the final match of the Andersen Consulting Match Play in February and Sutton in The Players Championship the following month. Both Clarke and Sutton played exceptionally well those two weeks. But remember, both men had to deal with Woods. He seems to play exceptionally well every week.

Looking at Woods' potential, Nick Price expressed sympathy for the men playing against him, saying, "I feel sorry for the young guys."

With Woods' stature, it is only natural that he should be compared with Jack Nicklaus, who was certainly among the very best who have played the game. Nicklaus lasted more than 20 years; by the year 2000, Woods had lasted only four, and yet the other players confess they're in awe of him.

Rocco Mediate said, "We're all mortal. He's not."

Is that good? Tom Kite doesn't think it is.

"You need competition. Otherwise it gets boring," he said.

Meantime, Woods has kept himself above the debate, more concerned with savoring the moment.

"I'll appreciate this a lot more in the future, because I'm too close to it at the moment. I can't tell you historically what it really means. Even when I won the Masters, it took me two or three years to understand what I had done."

It may take the rest of us longer to grasp what has happened. We do know that one of Kite's comments is indeed true:

"Tiger needs to be pushed."

In the frenzy to acclaim Woods' accomplishment, it is possible, however, it may have been

"I'll appreciate this a lot more in the future," Woods said, "because I'm too close to it at the moment."

overdone. We seem to forget that when Woods won the 1997 Masters by shooting 270, he shaved Nicklaus' record by only one stroke. Jack had shot 271 in 1965.

Remember, too, that Nicklaus hit the ball amazing distances as well. Playing Augusta's 15th hole one day in 1965, the year he set his record, he must have driven his ball more than 300 yards. Sizing up his approach, Nicklaus chose an 8-iron and almost hit it into the pond at the 16th. Asked why he didn't play a shorter club, Nicklaus replied rather sheepishly, "I'd have felt stupid hitting a 9-iron."

Don't forget: Like everyone else in those days, he was playing a persimmon driver with a steel shaft and a wound balata ball with 342 dimples.

Nicklaus won that Masters by nine strokes, but we didn't hear someone like Byron Nelson or Ben Hogan, or Jimmy Demaret, or Gene Sarazen saying they felt sorry for the younger players. Arnold Palmer had finished second. Can you imagine Palmer asking how he could cope with a guy who drives the ball 300 yards and plays 9-irons into par-5 holes? Ernie Els asked that question at Pebble Beach.

Yes, Nicklaus beat Palmer that week, but don't think for a second that Palmer didn't *know* he could beat Nicklaus any day Jack wanted to play.

Where have the Arnold Palmers gone? Were there any around to challenge Woods when the 20th century wound down? Where were the Gary Players, the Billy Caspers, the Lee Trevinos or the Tom Watsons, the men who pushed Nicklaus?

When Nicklaus kept beating them did he so demoralize them they wailed they were mortal but he wasn't? Trevino always called Nicklaus the greatest player who ever lived, but everyone knew he finished the sentence by adding silently, "but I can beat him."

Years may pass before we know if any of our modern heroes have their ability, their self-assurance and their determination. Or do we have instead a very large band of players who surface briefly, then fade away?

That is speculation. In the meantime, Woods left no reason to guess about his immediate plans.

"I've got the trophy," he said. "Now I get to go home."

100th U.S. OPEN Pebble Beach

June 15-18, 2000, Pebble Beach Golf Links, Pebble Beach, Calif.

Contestant		Rounds			Total	Prize
Tiger Woods	65	69	71	67	272	$800,000.00
Miguel Angel Jimenez	66	74	76	71	287	390,150.00
Ernie Els	74	73	68	72	287	390,150.00
John Huston	67	75	76	70	288	212,779.00
Lee Westwood	71	71	76	71	289	162,526.00
Padraig Harrington	73	71	72	73	289	162,526.00
Nick Faldo	69	74	76	71	290	137,203.00
Vijay Singh	70	73	80	68	291	112,766.00
Stewart Cink	77	72	72	70	291	112,766.00
David Duval	75	71	74	71	291	112,766.00
Loren Roberts	68	78	73	72	291	112,766.00
Paul Azinger	71	73	79	69	292	86,223.00
Retief Goosen	77	72	72	71	292	86,223.00
Michael Campbell	71	77	71	73	292	86,223.00
Jose Maria Olazabal	70	71	76	75	292	86,223.00
Mike Weir	76	72	76	69	293	65,214.00
Scott Hoch	73	76	75	69	293	65,214.00
Justin Leonard	73	73	75	72	293	65,214.00
David Toms	73	76	72	72	293	65,214.00
Fred Couples	70	75	75	73	293	65,214.00
Phil Mickelson	71	73	73	76	293	65,214.00
Notah Begay III	74	75	72	73	294	53,105.00
Hal Sutton	69	73	83	70	295	45,537.00
Mike Brisky	71	73	79	72	295	45,537.00
Bob May	72	76	75	72	295	45,537.00
Tom Lehman	71	73	78	73	295	45,537.00
Hale Irwin	68	78	81	69	296	34,066.00
Nick Price	77	70	78	71	296	34,066.00
Steve Stricker	75	74	75	72	296	34,066.00
Tom Watson	71	74	78	73	296	34,066.00
Steve Jones	75	73	75	73	296	34,066.00
Richard Zokol	74	74	80	69	297	28,247.00
Lee Porter	74	70	83	70	297	28,247.00
Tom Kite	72	77	77	71	297	28,247.00
Christopher Perry	75	72	78	72	297	28,247.00
Rocco Mediate	69	76	75	77	297	28,247.00
Jerry Kelly	73	73	81	71	298	22,056.00
Woody Austin	77	70	78	73	298	22,056.00
Angel Cabrera	69	76	79	74	298	22,056.00
Charles Warren	75	74	75	74	298	22,056.00
Ted Tryba	71	73	79	75	298	22,056.00
Lee Janzen	71	73	79	75	298	22,056.00
Craig Parry	73	74	76	75	298	22,056.00
Bobby Clampett	68	77	76	77	298	22,056.00

100th U.S. Open

Contestant	Rounds				Total	Prize
Larry Mize	73	72	76	77	298	22,056.00
Sergio Garcia	75	71	81	72	299	15,891.00
Colin Montgomerie	73	74	79	73	299	15,891.00
Scott Verplank	72	74	78	75	299	15,891.00
Rick Hartmann	73	75	75	76	299	15,891.00
Thomas Bjorn	70	70	82	77	299	15,891.00
Mark O'Meara	74	74	78	74	300	13,578.00
Warren Schutte	74	75	74	77	300	13,578.00
Darren Clarke	71	75	83	72	301	12,747.00
Keith Clearwater	74	74	80	73	301	12,747.00
Jeff Coston	70	77	80	74	301	12,747.00
Kirk Triplett	70	71	84	77	302	12,153.00
Jimmy Green	74	75	77	77	303	11,760.00
Dave Eichelberger	78	69	77	79	303	11,760.00
*Jeffrey Wilson	74	72	82	76	304	Medal
Jim Furyk	72	74	84	75	305	11,425.00
Brandel Chamblee	70	77	82	77	306	11,144.00
Carlos Franco	74	75	75	82	306	11,144.00
Robert Damron	72	73	84	84	313	10,862.00

Mike Burke, Jr.	77	73	150	Edward Fryatt	78	74	152	Cameron Beckman	78	78	156
Corey Pavin	72	78	150	Jonathan Kaye	74	78	152	Brad Elder	79	77	156
Dudley Hart	77	73	150	Jean Van de Velde	76	76	152	Brad Faxon	80	76	156
Bob Estes	73	77	150	Jeff Sluman	78	74	152	Taggart Ridings	80	76	156
Don Pooley	76	74	150	*Ricky Barnes	80	73	153	*Craig Lile	78	78	156
Ryuji Imada	75	75	150	Paul Goydos	71	82	153	Jarmo Sandelin	77	80	157
Brian Gay	72	78	150	Andrew Magee	74	79	153	Bernhard Langer	77	80	157
Fred Funk	76	74	150	Brett Quigley	75	78	153	Ed Whitman	82	75	157
Brian Henninger	77	73	150	Chris Tidland	77	76	153	Shigeki Maruyama	77	80	157
Kevin Johnson	74	76	150	Jesper Parnevik	73	80	153	Glen Day	77	80	157
Tim Herron	75	75	150	*Aaron Baddeley	79	74	153	Mike Malizia	76	81	157
Todd Fischer	78	72	150	Steve Pate	74	80	154	Jeff Lee	79	78	157
Dennis Paulson	75	76	151	Robert Gamez	75	79	154	Jon Levitt	79	78	157
Jeff Maggert	72	79	151	Davis Love III	75	79	154	Frank Lickliter II	81	77	158
Stuart Appleby	75	76	151	David Berganio, Jr.	77	77	154	*Jedd McLuen	79	79	158
Frank Nobilo	75	76	151	Andy Bean	77	77	154	Billy Mayfair	83	75	158
Tommy Armour III	76	75	151	Rory Sabbatini	79	75	154	Jim Carter	76	82	158
Matt Gogel	72	79	151	Mike Borich	77	77	154	Greg Norman	77	82	159
Mark Slawter	77	74	151	Jason Buha	80	75	155	J.L. Lewis	77	82	159
Chris Kaufman	76	75	151	Jake Reeves	74	81	155	Craig Spence	76	83	159
Mark Brooks	74	77	151	*David Gossett	78	77	155	Rick Stimmel	76	83	159
Brent Geiberger	73	78	151	Jack Nicklaus	73	82	155	Mario Tiziani	80	79	159
Bill Van Orman	76	75	151	J.P. Hayes	76	79	155	Rodney Butcher	84	75	159
Chad Campbell	74	77	151	John Cook	79	76	155	Mike Troy	79	81	160
Craig Stadler	79	72	151	Michael Harris	77	78	155	Graham Davidson	81	79	160
Brandt Jobe	72	79	151	*Andrew Sanders	77	78	155	Ken Krieger	81	79	160
Duffy Waldorf	73	78	151	Kyle Blackman	78	77	155	Rick Heath	79	81	160
David Frost	76	76	152	Zoran Zorkic	80	76	156	Clark Renner	85	76	161
Darrell Kestner	74	78	152	Paul Gow	77	79	156	Curtis Strange	81	81	162
Joe Daley	83	69	152	Scott Gump	74	82	156	Colin Amaral	79	83	162
Jim McGovern	76	76	152	Javier Sanchez	77	79	156	John Daly	83		WD

Professionals not returning 72-hole scores received $1,000 each.   *Denotes amateur.

100th U.S. OPEN Statistics

Hole	1	2	3	4	5	6	7	8	9	10	11	12	13	14	15	16	17	18	Total	
Par	4	4	4	4	3	5	3	4	4	4	4	3	4	5	4	4	3	5	71	
Tiger Woods																				
Round 1	4	4	4	③	3	5	②	4	4	③	4	3	③	④	4	4	3	④	65	
Round 2	4	4	③	4	[4]	④	②	4	[5]	4	③	②	4	[6]	③	4	3	[6]	69	
Round 3	4	③	[7]	4	3	④	②	[5]	③	[5]	4	3	4	④	4	4	3	5	71	
Round 4	4	4	4	4	3	5	3	4	4	③	4	②	③	④	4	4	3	5	67	272
Miguel Angel Jimenez																				
Round 1	4	③	③	4	②	④	②	4	[5]	4	③	3	4	5	[5]	4	3	④	66	
Round 2	4	4	4	4	3	④	3	[5]	4	[5]	[5]	[4]	4	5	4	4	[4]	④	74	
Round 3	[5]	4	4	4	[4]	5	3	[5]	4	4	4	3	4	5	4	[5]	[4]	5	76	
Round 4	③	4	4	4	②	④	3	4	[5]	4	4	3	4	5	4	4	[4]	[6]	71	287
Ernie Els																				
Round 1	4	4	4	4	[4]	④	②	4	4	4	4	[4]	[5]	5	[5]	[5]	3	5	74	
Round 2	4	4	4	4	3	5	3	4	4	[5]	[5]	[4]	4	④	4	4	3	5	73	
Round 3	4	4	4	4	②	3	④	[4]	[5]	4	4	③	3	[5]	④	③	4	3	5	68	
Round 4	4	4	4	4	[5]	[4]	5	3	4	③	③	4	[4]	4	5	4	4	3	5	72	287
John Huston																				
Round 1	③	[5]	③	4	3	④	②	[5]	4	③	③	3	[5]	5	③	4	3	5	67	
Round 2	4	[7]	4	③	3	④	3	4	[6]	4	③	[4]	[5]	[6]	③	[5]	3	④	75	
Round 3	4	[5]	[5]	[5]	3	5	②	[5]	4	4	[5]	[4]	4	④	4	[5]	②	[6]	76	
Round 4	[5]	[5]	③	③	②	5	3	4	4	4	③	[4]	4	5	4	4	3	5	70	288

○ Circled numbers represent birdies or eagles. □ Squared numbers represent bogeys or worse.

Hole	Yards	Par	Eagles	Birdies	Pars	Bogeys	Double Bogeys	Higher	Average
1	381	4	1	46	285	96	8	0	4.147
2	484	4	0	28	221	167	16	4	4.420
3	390	4	0	54	256	107	16	3	4.216
4	331	4	1	97	273	55	10	0	3.945
5	188	3	0	27	245	138	23	3	3.381
6	524	5	6	137	227	60	4	2	4.830
7	106	3	1	70	288	68	8	1	3.034
8	418	4	0	24	208	162	35	7	4.534
9	466	4	0	16	212	165	37	6	4.557
OUT	3,288	35	9	499	2,215	1,018	157	26	37.064
10	446	4	0	44	225	128	35	4	4.383
11	380	4	0	50	275	102	9	0	4.161
12	202	3	0	16	259	151	9	1	3.360
13	406	4	0	58	278	92	8	0	4.115
14	573	5	0	33	235	141	25	2	5.376
15	397	4	2	59	294	72	8	1	4.064
16	403	4	0	34	256	127	16	3	4.307
17	208	3	0	17	238	157	22	2	3.436
18	543	5	2	107	221	81	16	9	5.089
IN	3,558	36	4	418	2,281	1,051	148	22	38.291
TOTAL	6,846	71	13	917	4,496	2,069	305	48	75.355

100th U.S. OPEN Past Results

Date	Winner	Score	Runner-Up	Venue
1895	Horace Rawlins	173 - 36 holes	Willie Dunn	Newport GC, Newport, RI
1896	James Foulis	152 - 36 holes	Horace Rawlins	Shinnecock Hills GC, Southampton, NY
1897	Joe Lloyd	162 - 36 holes	Willie Anderson	Chicago GC, Wheaton, IL
1898	Fred Herd	328 - 72 holes	Alex Smith	Myopia Hunt Club, S. Hamilton, MA
1899	Willie Smith	315	George Low / Val Fitzjohn / W.H. Way	Baltimore CC, Baltimore, MD
1900	Harry Vardon	313	J.H. Taylor	Chicago GC, Wheaton, IL
1901	*Willie Anderson (85)	331	Alex Smith (86)	Myopia Hunt Club, S. Hamilton, MA
1902	Laurie Auchterlonie	307	Stewart Gardner	Garden City GC, Garden City, NY
1903	*Willie Anderson (82)	307	David Brown (84)	Baltusrol GC, Springfield, NJ
1904	Willie Anderson	303	Gil Nicholls	Glen View Club, Golf, IL
1905	Willie Anderson	314	Alex Smith	Myopia Hunt Club, S. Hamilton, MA
1906	Alex Smith	295	Willie Smith	Onwentsia Club, Lake Forest, IL
1907	Alex Ross	302	Gil Nicholls	Philadelphia Cricket Club, Chestnut Hill, PA
1908	*Fred McLeod (77)	322	Willie Smith (83)	Myopia Hunt Club, S. Hamilton, MA
1909	George Sargent	290	Tom McNamara	Englewood GC, Englewood, NJ
1910	*Alex Smith (71) / Macdonald Smith (77)	298	John J. McDermott (75)	Philadelphia Cricket Club, Chestnut Hill, PA
1911	*John J. McDermott (80)	307	Michael J. Brady (82) / George O. Simpson (85)	Chicago GC, Wheaton, IL
1912	John J. McDermott	294	Tom McNamara	CC of Buffalo, Buffalo, NY
1913	*Francis Ouimet (72)	304	Harry Vardon (77) / Edward Ray (78)	The Country Club, Brookline, MA
1914	Walter Hagen	290	Charles Evans, Jr.	Midlothian CC, Blue Island, IL
1915	Jerome D. Travers	297	Tom McNamara	Baltusrol GC, Springfield, NJ
1916	Charles Evans, Jr.	286	Jock Hutchinson	Minikahda Club, Minneapolis, MN
1917-18	No Championships Played — World War I			
1919	*Walter Hagen (77)	301	Michael J. Brady (78)	Brae Burn CC, West Newton, MA
1920	Edward Ray	295	Harry Vardon / Jack Burke, Sr. / Leo Diegel / Jock Hutchison	Inverness Club, Toledo, OH
1921	James M. Barnes	289	Walter Hagen / Fred McLeod	Columbia CC, Chevy Chase, MD
1922	Gene Sarazen	288	John L. Black / Robert T. Jones, Jr.	Skokie CC, Glencoe, IL
1923	*Robert T. Jones, Jr. (76)	296	Bobby Cruickshank (78)	Inwood CC, Inwood, NY
1924	Cyril Walker	297	Robert T. Jones, Jr.	Oakland Hills CC, Birmingham, MI
1925	*William MacFarlane (147)	291	Robert T. Jones, Jr. (148)	Worcester CC, Worcester, MA
1926	Robert T. Jones, Jr.	293	Joe Turnesa	Scioto CC, Columbus, OH
1927	*Tommy Armour (76)	301	Harry Cooper (79)	Oakmont CC, Oakmont, PA
1928	*Johnny Farrell (143)	294	Robert T. Jones, Jr. (144)	Olympia Fields CC, Matteson, IL
1929	*Robert T. Jones, Jr. (141)	294	Al Espinosa (164)	Winged Foot GC, Mamaroneck, NY
1930	Robert T. Joncs, Jr.	287	Macdonald Smith	Interlachen CC, Hopkins, MN

Past Results

Date	Winner	Score	Runner-Up	Venue
1931	*Billy Burke (149-148)	292	George Von Elm (149-149)	Inverness Club, Toledo, OH
1932	Gene Sarazen	286	Phil Perkins Bobby Cruickshank	Fresh Meadows CC, Flushing, NY
1933	Johnny Goodman	287	Ralph Guldahl	North Shore CC, Glenview, IL
1934	Olin Dutra	293	Gene Sarazen	Merion Cricket Club, Ardmore, PA
1935	Sam Parks, Jr.	299	Jimmy Thomson	Oakmont CC, Oakmont, PA
1936	Tony Manero	282	Harry Cooper	Baltusrol GC, Springfield, NJ
1937	Ralph Guldahl	281	Sam Snead	Oakland Hills CC, Birmingham, MI
1938	Ralph Guldahl	284	Dick Metz	Cherry Hills CC, Englewood, CO
1939	*Byron Nelson (68-70)	284	Craig Wood (68-73) Denny Shute (76)	Philadelphia CC, West Conshohocken, PA
1940	*Lawson Little (70)	287	Gene Sarazen (73)	Canterbury GC, Cleveland, OH
1941	Craig Wood	284	Denny Shute	Colonial Club, Fort Worth, TX
1942-45	No Championships Played — World War II			
1946	*Lloyd Mangrum (72-72)	284	Vic Ghezzi (72-73) Byron Nelson (72-73)	Canterbury GC, Cleveland, OH
1947	*Lew Worsham (69)	282	Sam Snead (70)	St. Louis CC, Clayton, MO
1948	Ben Hogan	276	Jimmy Demaret	Riviera CC, Los Angeles, CA
1949	Cary Middlecoff	286	Sam Snead Clayton Heafner	Medinah CC, Medinah, IL
1950	*Ben Hogan (69)	287	Lloyd Mangrum (73) George Fazio (75)	Merion GC, Ardmore, PA
1951	Ben Hogan	287	Clayton Heafner	Oakland Hills CC, Birmingham, MI
1952	Julius Boros	281	Ed (Porky) Oliver	Northwood CC, Dallas, TX
1953	Ben Hogan	283	Sam Snead	Oakmont CC, Oakmont, PA
1954	Ed Furgol	284	Gene Littler	Baltusrol GC, Springfield, NJ
1955	*Jack Fleck (69)	287	Ben Hogan (72)	The Olympic Club, San Francisco, CA
1956	Cary Middlecoff	281	Ben Hogan Julius Boros	Oak Hill CC, Rochester, NY
1957	*Dick Mayer (72)	282	Cary Middlecoff (79)	Inverness Club, Toledo, OH
1958	Tommy Bolt	283	Gary Player	Southern Hills CC, Tulsa, OK
1959	Billy Casper	282	Bob Rosburg	Winged Foot GC, Mamaroneck, NY
1960	Arnold Palmer	280	Jack Nicklaus	Cherry Hills CC, Englewood, CO
1961	Gene Littler	281	Bob Goalby Doug Sanders	Oakland Hills CC, Birmingham, MI
1962	*Jack Nicklaus (71)	283	Arnold Palmer (74)	Oakmont CC, Oakmont, PA
1963	*Julius Boros (70)	293	Jacky Cupit (73) Arnold Palmer (76)	The Country Club, Brookline, MA
1964	Ken Venturi	278	Tommy Jacobs	Congressional CC, Bethesda, MD
1965	*Gary Player (71)	282	Kel Nagle (74)	Bellerive CC, St. Louis, MO
1966	*Billy Casper (69)	278	Arnold Palmer (73)	The Olympic Club, San Francisco, CA
1967	Jack Nicklaus	275	Arnold Palmer	Baltusrol GC, Springfield, NJ
1968	Lee Trevino	275	Jack Nicklaus	Oak Hill CC, Rochester, NY
1969	Orville Moody	281	Deane Beman Al Geiberger Bob Rosburg	Champions GC, Houston, TX
1970	Tony Jacklin	281	Dave Hill	Hazeltine National GC, Chaska, MN
1971	*Lee Trevino (68)	280	Jack Nicklaus (71)	Merion GC, Ardmore, PA
1972	Jack Nicklaus	290	Bruce Crampton	Pebble Beach GL, Pebble Beach, CA
1973	Johnny Miller	279	John Schlee	Oakmont CC, Oakmont, PA
1974	Hale Irwin	287	Forrest Fezler	Winged Foot GC, Mamaroneck, NY
1975	*Lou Graham (71)	287	John Mahaffey (73)	Medinah CC, Medinah, IL
1976	Jerry Pate	277	Tom Weiskopf Al Geiberger	Atlanta Athletic Club, Duluth, GA

100th U.S. Open

Date	Winner	Score	Runner-Up	Venue
1977	Hubert Green	278	Lou Graham	Southern Hills CC, Tulsa, OK
1978	Andy North	285	Dave Stockton J.C. Snead	Cherry Hills CC, Englewood, CO
1979	Hale Irwin	284	Gary Player Jerry Pate	Inverness Club, Toledo, OH
1980	Jack Nicklaus	272	Isao Aoki	Baltusrol GC, Springfield, NJ
1981	David Graham	273	George Burns Bill Rogers	Merion GC, Ardmore, PA
1982	Tom Watson	282	Jack Nicklaus	Pebble Beach GL, Pebble Beach, CA
1983	Larry Nelson	280	Tom Watson	Oakmont CC, Oakmont, PA
1984	*Fuzzy Zoeller (67)	276	Greg Norman (75)	Winged Foot GC, Mamaroneck, NY
1985	Andy North	279	Dave Barr Chen Tze Chung Denis Watson	Oakland Hills CC, Birmingham, MI
1986	Raymond Floyd	279	Lanny Wadkins Chip Beck	Shinnecock Hills GC, Southampton, NY
1987	Scott Simpson	277	Tom Watson	The Olympic Club, San Francisco, CA
1988	*Curtis Strange (71)	278	Nick Faldo (75)	The Country Club, Brookline, MA
1989	Curtis Strange	278	Chip Beck Mark McCumber Ian Woosnam	Oak Hill CC, Rochester, NY
1990	*Hale Irwin (74+3)	280	Mike Donald (74+4)	Medinah CC, Medinah, IL
1991	*Payne Stewart (75)	282	Scott Simpson (77)	Hazeltine National GC, Chaska, MN
1992	Tom Kite	285	Jeff Sluman	Pebble Beach GL, Pebble Beach, CA
1993	Lee Janzen	272	Payne Stewart	Baltusrol GC, Springfield, NJ
1994	*Ernie Els (74+4+4)	279	Loren Roberts (74+4+5) Colin Montgomerie (78)	Oakmont CC, Oakmont, PA
1995	Corey Pavin	280	Greg Norman	Shinnecock Hills GC, Southampton, NY
1996	Steve Jones	278	Tom Lehman Davis Love III	Oakland Hills CC, Birmingham, MI
1997	Ernie Els	276	Colin Montgomerie	Congressional CC, Bethesda, MD
1998	Lee Janzen	280	Payne Stewart	The Olympic Club, San Francisco, CA
1999	Payne Stewart	279	Phil Mickelson	Pinehurst No. 2, Pinehurst, NC
2000	Tiger Woods	272	Miguel Angel Jimenez Ernie Els	Pebble Beach GL, Pebble Beach, CA

*Winner in playoff; figures in parentheses indicate scores

100th U.S. OPEN Championship Records

Oldest champion (years/months/days)
   45/0/15 — Hale Irwin (1990)
Youngest champion
   19/10/14 — John J. McDermott (1911)
Most victories
   4 — Willie Anderson (1901, '03, '04, '05)
   4 — Robert T. Jones, Jr. (1923, '26, '29, '30)
   4 — Ben Hogan (1948, '50, '51, '53)
   4 — Jack Nicklaus (1962, '67, '72, '80)
   3 — Hale Irwin (1974, '79, '90)
   2 — by 14 players: Alex Smith (1906, '10), John J. McDermott (1911, '12), Walter Hagen (1914, '19), Gene Sarazen (1922, '32), Ralph Guldahl (1937, '38), Cary Middlecoff (1949, '56), Julius Boros (1952, '63), Billy Casper (1959, '66), Lee Trevino (1968, '71), Andy North (1978, '85), Curtis Strange (1988, '89), Ernie Els (1994, '97), Lee Janzen (1993, '98), and Payne Stewart (1991, '99).
Consecutive victories
   Willie Anderson (1903, '04, '05)
   John J. McDermott (1911, '12)
   Robert T. Jones, Jr. (1929, '30)
   Ralph Guldahl (1937, '38)
   Ben Hogan (1950, '51)
   Curtis Strange (1988, '89)
Most times runner-up
   4 — Sam Snead
   4 — Robert T. Jones, Jr.
   4 — Arnold Palmer
   4 — Jack Nicklaus
Longest course
   7,213 yards — Congressional CC, Bethesda, MD (1997)
Shortest course
   Since World War II
   6,528 yards — Merion GC (East Course), Ardmore, PA (1971, '81)
Most often host club of Open
   7 — Baltusrol GC, Springfield, NJ (1903, '15, '36, '54, '67, '80, '93)
   7 — Oakmont (PA) CC (1927, '35, '53, '62, '73, '83, '94)
Largest entry
   8,457 (2000)
Smallest entry
   11 (1895)
Lowest score, 72 holes
   272 — Jack Nicklaus (63-71-70-68), at Baltusrol GC (Lower Course), Springfield, NJ (1980)
   272 — Lee Janzen (67-67-69-69), at Baltusrol GC (Lower Course), Springfield, NJ (1993)
   272 — Tiger Woods (65-69-71-67), at Pebble Beach GL, Pebble Beach, CA (2000)

Lowest score, first 54 holes
   203 — George Burns (69-66-68), at Merion GC (East Course), Ardmore, PA (1981)
   203 — Tze-Chung Chen (65-69-69), at Oakland Hills CC (South Course), Birmingham, MI (1985)
   203 — Lee Janzen (67-67-69), at Baltusrol GC (Lower Course), Springfield, NJ (1993)
Lowest score, last 54 holes
   203 — Loren Roberts (69-64-70), at Oakmont CC, Oakmont, PA (1994)
Lowest score, first 36 holes
   134 — Jack Nicklaus (63-71), at Baltusrol GC (Lower Course), Springfield, NJ (1980)
   134 — Chen Tze-Chung (65-69), at Oakland Hills CC (South Course), Birmingham, MI (1985)
   134 — Lee Janzen (67-67), at Baltusrol GC (Lower Course), Springfield, NJ (1993)
   134 — Tiger Woods (65-69), at Pebble Beach GL, Pebble Beach, CA (2000)
Lowest score, last 36 holes
   132 — Larry Nelson (65-67), at Oakmont CC, Oakmont, PA (1983)
Lowest score, 9 holes
   29 — Neal Lancaster (second nine, fourth round) at Shinnecock Hills GC, Southampton, NY (1995)
   29 — Neal Lancaster (second nine, second round) at Oakland Hills CC, Birmingham, MI (1996)
Lowest score, 18 holes
   63 — Johnny Miller, fourth round at Oakmont CC, Oakmont, PA (1973)
   63 — Jack Nicklaus, first round at Baltusrol GC (Lower Course), Springfield, NJ (1980)
   63 — Tom Weiskopf, first round at Baltusrol GC (Lower Course), Springfield, NJ (1980)
Largest winning margin
   15 — Tiger Woods (272), at Pebble Beach GL, Pebble Beach CA (2000)
Highest winning score
   Since World War II
   293 — Julius Boros, at The Country Club, Brookline, MA (1963) (won in playoff)
Best start by champion
   63 — Jack Nicklaus, at Baltusrol GC (Lower Course), Springfield, NJ (1980)
Best finish by champion
   63 — Johnny Miller, at Oakmont (PA) CC (1973)
Worst start by champion
   Since World War II
   76 — Ben Hogan, at Oakland Hills CC (South Course), Birmingham, MI (1951)

Date	Winner	Score	Runner-Up	Venue
1977	Hubert Green	278	Lou Graham	Southern Hills CC, Tulsa, OK
1978	Andy North	285	Dave Stockton J.C. Snead	Cherry Hills CC, Englewood, CO
1979	Hale Irwin	284	Gary Player Jerry Pate	Inverness Club, Toledo, OH
1980	Jack Nicklaus	272	Isao Aoki	Baltusrol GC, Springfield, NJ
1981	David Graham	273	George Burns Bill Rogers	Merion GC, Ardmore, PA
1982	Tom Watson	282	Jack Nicklaus	Pebble Beach GL, Pebble Beach, CA
1983	Larry Nelson	280	Tom Watson	Oakmont CC, Oakmont, PA
1984	*Fuzzy Zoeller (67)	276	Greg Norman (75)	Winged Foot GC, Mamaroneck, NY
1985	Andy North	279	Dave Barr Chen Tze Chung Denis Watson	Oakland Hills CC, Birmingham, MI
1986	Raymond Floyd	279	Lanny Wadkins Chip Beck	Shinnecock Hills GC, Southampton, NY
1987	Scott Simpson	277	Tom Watson	The Olympic Club, San Francisco, CA
1988	*Curtis Strange (71)	278	Nick Faldo (75)	The Country Club, Brookline, MA
1989	Curtis Strange	278	Chip Beck Mark McCumber Ian Woosnam	Oak Hill CC, Rochester, NY
1990	*Hale Irwin (74+3)	280	Mike Donald (74+4)	Medinah CC, Medinah, IL
1991	*Payne Stewart (75)	282	Scott Simpson (77)	Hazeltine National GC, Chaska, MN
1992	Tom Kite	285	Jeff Sluman	Pebble Beach GL, Pebble Beach, CA
1993	Lee Janzen	272	Payne Stewart	Baltusrol GC, Springfield, NJ
1994	*Ernie Els (74+4+4)	279	Loren Roberts (74+4+5) Colin Montgomerie (78)	Oakmont CC, Oakmont, PA
1995	Corey Pavin	280	Greg Norman	Shinnecock Hills GC, Southampton, NY
1996	Steve Jones	278	Tom Lehman Davis Love III	Oakland Hills CC, Birmingham, MI
1997	Ernie Els	276	Colin Montgomerie	Congressional CC, Bethesda, MD
1998	Lee Janzen	280	Payne Stewart	The Olympic Club, San Francisco, CA
1999	Payne Stewart	279	Phil Mickelson	Pinehurst No. 2, Pinehurst, NC
2000	Tiger Woods	272	Miguel Angel Jimenez Ernie Els	Pebble Beach GL, Pebble Beach, CA

*Winner in playoff; figures in parentheses indicate scores

100th U.S. OPEN Championship Records

Oldest champion (years/months/days)
   45/0/15 — Hale Irwin (1990)
Youngest champion
   19/10/14 — John J. McDermott (1911)
Most victories
   4 — Willie Anderson (1901, '03, '04, '05)
   4 — Robert T. Jones, Jr. (1923, '26, '29, '30)
   4 — Ben Hogan (1948, '50, '51, '53)
   4 — Jack Nicklaus (1962, '67, '72, '80)
   3 — Hale Irwin (1974, '79, '90)
   2 — by 14 players: Alex Smith (1906, '10), John J. McDermott (1911, '12), Walter Hagen (1914, '19), Gene Sarazen (1922, '32), Ralph Guldahl (1937, '38), Cary Middlecoff (1949, '56), Julius Boros (1952, '63), Billy Casper (1959, '66), Lee Trevino (1968, '71), Andy North (1978, '85), Curtis Strange (1988, '89), Ernie Els (1994, '97), Lee Janzen (1993, '98), and Payne Stewart (1991, '99).
Consecutive victories
   Willie Anderson (1903, '04, '05)
   John J. McDermott (1911, '12)
   Robert T. Jones, Jr. (1929, '30)
   Ralph Guldahl (1937, '38)
   Ben Hogan (1950, '51)
   Curtis Strange (1988, '89)
Most times runner-up
   4 — Sam Snead
   4 — Robert T. Jones, Jr.
   4 — Arnold Palmer
   4 — Jack Nicklaus
Longest course
   7,213 yards — Congressional CC, Bethesda, MD (1997)
Shortest course
   Since World War II
   6,528 yards — Merion GC (East Course), Ardmore, PA (1971, '81)
Most often host club of Open
   7 — Baltusrol GC, Springfield, NJ (1903, '15, '36, '54, '67, '80, '93)
   7 — Oakmont (PA) CC (1927, '35, '53, '62, '73, '83, '94)
Largest entry
   8,457 (2000)
Smallest entry
   11 (1895)
Lowest score, 72 holes
   272 — Jack Nicklaus (63-71-70-68), at Baltusrol GC (Lower Course), Springfield, NJ (1980)
   272 — Lee Janzen (67-67-69-69), at Baltusrol GC (Lower Course), Springfield, NJ (1993)
   272 — Tiger Woods (65-69-71-67), at Pebble Beach GL, Pebble Beach, CA (2000)

Lowest score, first 54 holes
   203 — George Burns (69-66-68), at Merion GC (East Course), Ardmore, PA (1981)
   203 — Tze-Chung Chen (65-69-69), at Oakland Hills CC (South Course), Birmingham, MI (1985)
   203 — Lee Janzen (67-67-69), at Baltusrol GC (Lower Course), Springfield, NJ (1993)
Lowest score, last 54 holes
   203 — Loren Roberts (69-64-70), at Oakmont CC, Oakmont, PA (1994)
Lowest score, first 36 holes
   134 — Jack Nicklaus (63-71), at Baltusrol GC (Lower Course), Springfield, NJ (1980)
   134 — Chen Tze-Chung (65-69), at Oakland Hills CC (South Course), Birmingham, MI (1985)
   134 — Lee Janzen (67-67), at Baltusrol GC (Lower Course), Springfield, NJ (1993)
   134 — Tiger Woods (65-69), at Pebble Beach GL, Pebble Beach, CA (2000)
Lowest score, last 36 holes
   132 — Larry Nelson (65-67), at Oakmont CC, Oakmont, PA (1983)
Lowest score, 9 holes
   29 — Neal Lancaster (second nine, fourth round) at Shinnecock Hills GC, Southampton, NY (1995)
   29 — Neal Lancaster (second nine, second round) at Oakland Hills CC, Birmingham, MI (1996)
Lowest score, 18 holes
   63 — Johnny Miller, fourth round at Oakmont CC, Oakmont, PA (1973)
   63 — Jack Nicklaus, first round at Baltusrol GC (Lower Course), Springfield, NJ (1980)
   63 — Tom Weiskopf, first round at Baltusrol GC (Lower Course), Springfield, NJ (1980)
Largest winning margin
   15 — Tiger Woods (272), at Pebble Beach GL, Pebble Beach CA (2000)
Highest winning score
   Since World War II
   293 — Julius Boros, at The Country Club, Brookline, MA (1963) (won in playoff)
Best start by champion
   63 — Jack Nicklaus, at Baltusrol GC (Lower Course), Springfield, NJ (1980)
Best finish by champion
   63 — Johnny Miller, at Oakmont (PA) CC (1973)
Worst start by champion
   Since World War II
   76 — Ben Hogan, at Oakland Hills CC (South Course), Birmingham, MI (1951)

76 — Jack Fleck, at The Olympic Club (Lake Course), San Francisco, CA (1955)

Worst finish by champion
Since World War II
75 — Cary Middlecoff, at Medinah CC (No. 3 Course), Medinah, IL (1949)
75 — Hale Irwin, at Inverness Club, Toledo, OH (1979)

Lowest score to lead field, 18 holes
63 — Jack Nicklaus and Tom Weiskopf, at Baltusrol GC (Lower Course), Springfield, NJ (1980)

Lowest score to lead field, 36 holes
134 — Jack Nicklaus (63-71), at Baltusrol GC (Lower Course), Springfield, NJ (1980)
134 — Chen Tze-Chung (65-69), at Oakland Hills CC (South Course), Birmingham, MI (1985)
134 — Lee Janzen (67-67), at Baltusrol GC (Lower Course), Springfield, NJ (1993)
134 — Tiger Woods (65-69), at Pebble Beach GL, Pebble Beach, CA (2000)

Lowest score to lead field, 54 holes
203 — George Burns (69-66-68), at Merion GC (East Course), Ardmore, PA (1981)
203 — Chen Tze-Chung (65-69-69), at Oakland Hills CC (South Course), Birmingham, MI (1985)
203 — Lee Janzen (67-67-69), at Baltusrol GC (Lower Course), Springfield, NJ (1993)

Highest score to lead field, 18 holes
Since World War II
71 — Sam Snead, at Oakland Hills CC (South Course), Birmingham, MI (1951)
71 — Tommy Bolt, Julius Boros, and Dick Metz, at Southern Hills CC, Tulsa, OK (1958)
71 — Tony Jacklin, at Hazeltine National GC, Chaska, MN (1970)
71 — Orville Moody, Jack Nicklaus, Chi Chi Rodriguez, Mason Rudolph, Tom Shaw, and Kermit Zarley, at Pebble Beach (CA) Golf Links (1972)

Highest score to lead field, 36 holes
Since World War II
144 — Bobby Locke (73-71), at Oakland Hills CC (South Course), Birmingham, MI (1951)
144 — Tommy Bolt (67-77) and E. Harvie Ward (74-70), at The Olympic Club (Lake Course), San Francisco, CA (1955)
144 — Homero Blancas (74-70), Bruce Crampton (74-70), Jack Nicklaus (71-73), Cesar Seduno (72-72), Lanny Wadkins (76-68) and Kermit Zarley (71-73), at Pebble Beach (CA) Golf Links (1972)

Highest score to lead field, 54 holes
Since World War II
218 — Bobby Locke (73-71-74), at Oakland Hills CC (South Course), Birmingham, MI (1951)
218 — Jacky Cupit (70-72-76), at The Country Club, Brookline, MA (1963)

Highest 36-hole cut
155 — at The Olympic Club (Lakeside Course), San Francisco, CA (1955)

Most players to tie for lead, 18 holes
7 — at Pebble Beach (CA) Golf Links (1972); at Southern Hills CC, Tulsa, OK (1977); and at Shinnecock Hills GC, Southampton, NY (1896)

Most players to tie for lead, 36 holes
6 — at Pebble Beach (CA) Golf Links (1972)

Most players to tie for lead, 54 holes
4 — at Oakmont (PA) CC (1973)

Most sub-par rounds, championship
124 — at Medinah CC (No. 3 Course), Medinah, IL (1990)

Most sub-par 72-hole totals, championship
28 — at Medinah CC (No. 3 Course), Medinah, IL (1990)

Most sub-par scores, first round
39 — at Medinah CC (No. 3 Course), Medinah, IL (1990)

Most sub-par scores, second round
47 — at Medinah CC (No. 3 Course), Medinah, IL (1990)

Most sub-par scores, third round
24 — at Medinah CC (No. 3 Course), Medinah, IL (1990)

Most sub-par scores, fourth round
18 — at Baltusrol GC (Lower Course), Springfield, NJ (1993)

Most sub-par rounds by one player in one championship
4 — Billy Casper, at The Olympic Club (Lakeside Course), San Francisco, CA (1966)
4 — Lee Trevino, at Oak Hill CC (East Course), Rochester, NY (1968)
4 — Tony Jacklin, at Hazeltine National GC, Chaska, MN (1970)
4 — Lee Janzen, at Baltusrol GC (Lower Course), Springfield, NJ (1993)

Highest score, one hole
19 — Ray Ainsley, at the 16th (par 4) at Cherry Hills CC, Englewood, CO (1938)

Most consecutive birdies
6 — George Burns (holes 2–7), at Pebble Beach (CA) Golf Links (1972) and Andy Dillard (holes 1-6), at Pebble Beach (CA) Golf Links (1992)

Most consecutive 3s
7 — Hubert Green (holes 10–16), at Southern Hills Country Club, Tulsa, OK (1977)
7 — Peter Jacobsen (holes 1–7), at The Country Club, Brookline, MA (1988)

Most consecutive Opens
44 — Jack Nicklaus (1957-2000)

Most Opens completed 72 holes
35 — Jack Nicklaus

Most consecutive Opens completed 72 holes
22 — Walter Hagen (1913-36; no Championships 1917-18)
22 — Gene Sarazen (1920-41)
22 — Gary Player (1958-79)

Robert Sommers is the former editor and publisher of the USGA's *Golf Journal*, author of *The U.S. Open: Golf's Ultimate Challenge* and *Golf Anecdotes*. He is based in Port St. Lucie, Fla.

Michael Cohen is a photographer based in New York City and a contributor to many magazines and books.

Fred Vuich is a staff photographer for *Golf Magazine*, a contributor to many books, and is based in Pittsburgh.

100th U.S. Open Championship
Pebble Beach Golf Links
June 15-18, 2000